A NEW BIRTH OF FREEDOM

A NEW BIRTH
OF FREEDOM

BY

NICHOLAS ROOSEVELT

Author of
The Restless Pacific
etc.

NEW YORK
CHARLES SCRIBNER'S SONS
1938

To

T. M. G. R.

CONTENTS

CONTENTS

"It is rather for us to be here dedicated to the great task remaining before us; . . . that we here highly resolve . . . that this nation under God shall have a new birth of freedom; and that government of the people, by the people, and for the people, shall not perish from the earth."

ABRAHAM LINCOLN: *Gettysburg Address.*

THE STRUGGLE FOR LIBERTY

I

MAN VS. AUTHORITY

For centuries brave men in the Western World fought
to free their fellows from the arbitrary dictates of their
rulers. They believed that certain rights of men are inalienable—that no government should ever be able to deny
them. Among these rights were freedom from unwarranted arrest, freedom to worship as they pleased, freedom to hold their own political opinions, and freedom in
their homes from the prying activities of government
agents and spies. To win these rights they curbed the
powers of government. They preserved these rights only
by being ever on guard against the subtle readiness of
political leaders to recapture lost privileges.

So successful were the champions of personal freedom
in Western Europe and North America that by the end
of the nineteenth century the civil liberties that they
had won had become deeply imbedded in the habits of
living and thinking of the peoples in these countries.
The concept of man as an inviolable personality, valuable for his own sake rather than for the sake of the
state, had triumphed. True, the rulers in Central and
Eastern Europe, the Orient and Latin America, had
resisted the demands for civil liberties. Men in these

regions remained little more than chattels. But in the English-speaking countries, and in France, Holland, Scandinavia, and Switzerland the rights of men to be free seemed unshakably established. That these countries contained only a small percentage of the world's population encouraged rather than discouraged fighters for civil liberties. Confident of ultimate victory, they planned to carry the struggle into new lands until all men everywhere should be free.

Today these rights are being flouted throughout the world. Men are being shot, imprisoned, tortured, robbed, oppressed, exiled, bullied, and silenced by government agents. The very ideal of liberty for which so many men died is being discredited, not only by cynical dictators but also by reformers. In its place the state-all-powerful is being proclaimed as the only hope for saving the world from its economic and social ills. The new creed asserts that the rights of individuals are neither inviolable nor valuable. Only society as a whole counts. Society, the reformers tell us, cannot survive unless men are made units in a perfectly functioning machine. Society must therefore devise a master plan, and through government, the members of society must be compelled to perform the tasks allotted to them by their leaders. Men's spiritual attributes, men's moral rights, have no significance. Their function, like those of bees, will be to carry out their prescribed work and die—to build the hive and help supply it with honey. They are to be mere tools, not personalities—little higher than the animals, and certainly much lower than the angels.

The mission of this state-all-powerful is to unify the economic activities of the nation so that all men shall have economic security. The perpetuation of this state requires that its mandates be carried out—even by coercion, if need be. The basis of this state is unlimited power placed unrestrained in the hands of its rulers. The inevitable tendency of this state will be to expand its powers of supervision and control until government interferes in even the least of human activities— interferes, of course, in the name of the interests of society as a whole. When society orders thus and so, the subject must obey. His interests, his rights, his ambitions, his dreams, count for nothing in comparison with the needs of the social hive.

This is rank reaction. The creation of a state-all-powerful means the return to the governors of those rights won from them throughout the long struggle for liberty. As Woodrow Wilson pointed out, the history of human freedom is the history of the limitation of governmental power, not its increase. It is the history of resistance. Liberty has never been the gift of government, but has been extorted from government by men who were willing to fight for what they believed to be their rights. To reverse this process—to give back to government as much power as the rulers demand—means to forfeit those personal rights already won. This has happened

5

in Germany, Italy, Russia, Japan. It is inevitable in any authoritarian state for the simple reason that civil liberties and government mastery cannot exist in the same nation at the same time. Civil liberties are, in fact, the denial of the right of government to be arbitrary—to step outside its proper sphere and tell each citizen what he may or must do. They deny the right of government to punish an individual for a purely political offense, as for example, opposition to the policy of the group in power. Paternalism, dictatorship, the authoritarian state, in contrast, rest on the power of government to dictate and compel, unhampered by laws and restraints. This power is held in check so long as civil liberties are still in force. Hence the task of those who favor the state-supreme is to seek to abolish civil liberties. If civil liberties can be preserved, dictatorship can be avoided. Create a collectivist state and these rights no longer can be exercised.

The more rational among the advocates of the state-all-powerful base their argument on the increasing complexity of modern society. In particular they say that the growth of vast corporate structures, which, though subordinate to the government, threaten to devour government, compels the state to be strong enough to hold them in check.

Obviously the more complex the social organization, the greater its need for restraining its members. But the distinction between restraint and regulation, on the one hand, and dictation and compulsion on the other, is fundamental. It is the distinction between liberty and servitude, between rules and orders. Regulation in the interest of the common good is largely negative. While it imposes restrictions which, until recent years, were primarily concerned with matters of public health and safety, it is not—or should not be—arbitrary. It assumes the willingness of free men to do voluntarily what is for the public good once they know what is required of them. It implies readiness to abide by the rules of the game. Compulsion, on the other hand, implies coercion— the use of force or the threat of force by government agents to compel men and women to do what the government wants regardless of the individual's wishes and rights.

When a state resorts to arbitrary compulsion, the beginning of the end of civil liberties is in sight. This is just as true if a state uses arbitrary compulsion with or without the approval of the majority of the voters. Arbitrary compulsion exercised in democracy is none the less liberty-depriving than in a dictatorship. What counts is not the form of government but how authority is exercised. The greater the state's authority to make men carry out some sort of plan or program the more it will have to resort to compulsion to make the people shoulder their share of the burden. When government is supreme the individual is a subject, no longer a citizen.

Liberty, the kind of liberty which Americans prized prior to the great depression, was the absence of arbitrary restraint. Americans have never resented reasonable regulations imposed in the interest of the community. They do not object to traffic rules and signals. In fact, they welcome them as aids to personal freedom of movement. But what everyone objects to is the arbitrary action of a traffic policeman who, out of personal whim or spite, arrests, insults and bullies a driver who has not knowingly violated a law. People will pay taxes—reluctantly. But they will not tolerate government interference in their intimate personal affairs. They refuse to accept government dictation as to how to run their businesses or farms.

This dislike of governmental meddling has its roots and its justification in American history. The Colonists revolted against arbitrary rulers. The framers of the Constitution devised many of the most important parts of that document in order to curtail the powers of government to interfere unreasonably in the proper conduct of a man's life. The first ten Amendments, now spoken of as the Bill of Rights, were added to the Constitution at the very inception of the Federal government in order still further to safeguard these personal rights.

Most Americans take these rights so much for granted that they are hardly aware of their existence, let alone their value and importance. Only when they read of men arrested, exiled and even killed in Europe for political reasons, and of religious persecution, or of press censorship, the seizure of letters and telegrams, the invasion of a man's home by government spies, or of persons who fear to comment on public affairs even in the privacy of their homes lest they be overheard and punished by those in power—only when Americans come to see that these are not isolated and rare occurrences but common incidents in whole sections of Europe, do they begin to glimpse the significance of the historic struggle to embody the elemental rights of man in indestructible form. It was as a check on arbitrary action by the rulers that these rights were originally proclaimed. Men believed these rights to be a guarantee against governmental injustice and tyranny. If the nazis had not abolished civil liberties in Germany the world would have been spared the shocking spectacle of the murder of General Schleicher and his wife on their own hearthstone by nazi agents. If civil liberties had existed in Soviet Russia wholesale political murders would not have been perpetrated.

In America the founding fathers were fully aware that these rights must be safeguarded by every possible means. Hence they sought to cement them in constitutional provisions which would bind governors and governed alike, making civil liberties secure for all time. Although they knew that mere legal recognition of these rights would not preserve them inviolable unless the people were willing to fight for them, they believed that posterity would share their own keen appreciation of the inestimable value of civil liberties. The founders were familiar with Aristotle's warning that if the citizens begin by giving up some part of the constitution, the government, with greater ease, will change something else which is a little more important until it has undermined the whole fabric of the state. But it did not occur to them that there would come a time when not only the rulers would reach out to recapture and revoke these rights of man, but the masses would resurrect the myth of the magic state and would turn to Uncle Sam, crying, "Save us!" They knew that no truer remark was ever made than that "eternal vigilance is the price of liberty." But the liberty which they transmitted to their heirs was so complete that the new generation took it as much for granted as wind and water, never dreaming that it could be snatched from them almost unawares. Was not liberty the birthright of every American? Was it not therefore safe for the ages?

The civil liberties which the founding fathers managed to assure—on paper—for those of us who have come after them include the following general provisions:

Freedom of person, which means freedom from arbitrary arrest, from enslavement and from the obligation to do forced labor. Men may not be arrested without due cause, or imprisoned or killed without a fair trial— in contrast to Germany and other authoritarian states.

Freedom of conscience, which implies the right to worship according to any sect and to practice any religious rites not in conflict with public morality.

Freedom of speech, which means to hold and to express such views on political and social questions as one wishes—with the proviso that one does not advocate the violent overthrow of government or affront public morals.

Freedom of the press, which includes the right to publish and to circulate all such opinions and criticisms as are not libellous or directly subversive of government.

Freedom of assembly, which means the right to gather together peaceably for public or other discussion.

Freedom from invasion of one's home by government agents except for due cause and with a special warrant.

Freedom from the unlawful seizure of one's papers, records, letters, telegrams, etc.

In addition the citizen has the right to elect officers, and, through his representatives, to participate in the making of laws, and the right to change the form of his government through constitutional amendment.

It would be foolish to pretend that these rights have not been abused by those in authority—particularly by local police and by minor state officials. Too often has freedom of assembly been questioned or denied, and the expression of political doctrines checked by menial minds moved by fear and false patriotism. The Federal Congress itself—and even the people, as witness the prohibition amendment—has not hesitated to infringe some of these rights from time to time. But no impartial student can deny that, taking it all in all, over a period of a century and a half, the civil liberties of the American people have been well and fairly kept. The real problem is to eliminate abuses and to prevent new powers being granted to those in office to deprive people of their civil liberties.

Those who assert that civil liberties have ceased to be valuable because there is no economic liberty except for the small fraction of families with incomes of over $3,000 a year, are muddying the waters of clear thinking. Civil liberties, as they have existed in Great Britain, the United States, and the British Dominions, have protected countless millions against political injustice. Economic liberty, in the sense that the term means escape from the need to work for a living, is the privilege of only a very few persons—men and women who have earned, appropriated or inherited wealth, and those who in one or other manner live at the expense of the government.

Economic freedom in the sense of a man's being able to work at whatever remunerative undertaking he likes is more restricted today than it was in America a century ago. Then a man with energy and acumen could work his way into almost any livelihood and, as a rule, failed or prospered according to his persistence and his luck. Today the opportunities of employment are more circumscribed by the location of great industrial centers, by specialization of occupation, and by the limitations on the ability or willingness of corporations to offer work. To this extent the individual's freedom of economic choice is more restricted in industrial America than it was in the rural civilization before 1850.

But economic freedom in the sense of opportunities for the acquisition of a substantial measure of financial independence is, if anything, commoner now than at any time during the last century. True, the chances for making a million are less. But to men of force, ability, character and the readiness to work more than eight hours a day many openings are still available which are almost certain to lead to substantial financial rewards. The demand for leaders, administrators, experts, has grown with the organization and technological improvements of modern business.

Remains today as ever the problem of those who have little more than their physical strength to use in the struggle for existence—those who are handicapped by lack of proper preparation for life. I do not include the shiftless and the idle by choice, as they form a comparatively small proportion of our population. But I do include many who have been described by politicians as the "underprivileged" or the "depressed third." They are the ones to whom economic freedom has no meaning. They are the ones who, in the present as in past societies, find the struggle to exist hardest. Too often they are life's dispossessed. Their ability to help themselves is so limited that dependence is—and has been—their traditional role.

Most of them know little and care less about their constitutional guarantees of civil liberties. But they would be the first to suffer in the event that civil liberties were to be curtailed for, in addition to their present economic misery, they would be subject to oppressive control by the state. The more the state assumes the role of economic master the greater its need for economic slaves. As in Russia, the "underprivileged" would merely exchange overlords—not gain new freedom. Experience in that country has proved that dictatorship of the proletariat is nothing but a flowery phrase for arbitrary control of a nation by a little clique of unscrupulous rulers. There is nothing but wishful thinking to show that such a clique could or would govern wisely and insure more of the good things of this world to more people. Economic freedom is unthinkable in an authoritarian state for the obvious reason that such a state must control the citizen as well as his means of livelihood, and that this state, if it is to survive, must force him to do his share of the nation's work.

In the long struggle of man against his governors the individual citizen is losing. Personal freedom is on the decline, and those who stand on the housetops and cry out that the world is backsliding into a new age of tyranny are ridiculed as reactionaries. What is liberty, cynical reformers ask, if it be but the freedom to starve?

"You can't eat the Constitution" was a byword in the depths of the depression. Therefore "Give us security," is the reformers' cry. "Feed us, clothe us, house us, warm us, light us, distract us," is the echo from a million tenements. If this can only be done by making government all-powerful, then give the rulers the powers they want. Provide steady work (not too hard), a modest wage, short hours, and benevolent protection against old age, unemployment, ill health and war and the people will gladly surrender all ambitions and all rights which may be demanded of them in the name of the state supreme.

Gone are the old ideals—gone, in fact, are any ideals, for the new creed of security is a coldly materialistic doctrine. It denies the teachings of religion and the value of things spiritual. It does not believe that anything is really worth fighting for. It is contemptuous of ambition, hope, and glory. It is indifferent to the arts. Man lives by bread alone, it insists, and anything more than the mere ministering to the flesh is superfluous. Work is a burden, effort futile, dreams idle. Freedom is a farce. What is needed is a planned society in which each person shall have the fixity of a cog—and shall perform work exactly as uncreative and uninspiring as that of a cog. Because a third of the population of the country is under-privileged we must raze the rest to a dead level, stifle initiative, penalize success and deride individuality. Only thus can enough security be assured to enough people. So runs the doctrine of dependence.

15

To those who hold these beliefs the Declaration of Independence is nothing but bombast and the soldiers who died at Valley Forge were fools. The framers of the Constitution were misguided self-seekers, and the men who made this country the haven of the oppressed and the hope of the downtrodden of the world were little more than pious frauds holding out vain promises. One and all were followers of false gods. They believed in men as free agents, as independent personalities, more important than society, superior to the state, whereas the new wisdom shows that society alone counts, and that whenever the major interests of society conflict with what men have heretofore regarded as their inalienable rights, men must give way to the state.

Here is the nub of the problem: Is the welfare of that somewhat mythical machine men call the state the supreme concern of society, or is the old ideal of the greatest good of the greatest number still worth fighting for? Are men henceforth to be mere tools, mere things, existing for the state, or have they rights which none but their Maker may curtail? Are they souls, not "hands" —persons with a spark of divine spirit, not mere robots —human beings with freedom to choose, or are they merely subjects without choice, destined to do as the state tells them? If the latter, the Statue of Liberty should be supplanted by a statue of security—a great cow with a thousand dugs, labelled the state supreme, with millions of men reaching out to obtain free milk.

16

II

GOVERNMENT, SERVANT OR MASTER?

GOVERNMENTS are of two major types—master or servant. Government either is unrestricted, and the rulers do as they wish, or it is limited and the rulers are subject to constitutional and legal restrictions and to removal by the governed.

There have been, of course, variations and combinations of these two types. But the distinction is fundamental. It is clearly illustrated in the contrast between the pre-war American form of government and Europe's post-war dictatorships. The American system was based on the consent of the governed—that is, on the theory that the people, through their elected representatives, could make and change the laws. The other system is based on the theory that the governors—not the people, but the group in power—know what is best for the country and that this group must not only make and enforce the laws but may change them at will. The American system rested on the conviction that men had certain rights which could not be taken from them. The other system asserts that men have no rights which government cannot at will override or modify.

The advocates of the master type of government have

a profound faith in the ignorance and incompetence of the masses. This is as true of present-day socialists and communists as it was of neolithic tribal chiefs. It is the rulers' duty to plan for and help the people. It is the people's duty to do as they are told. "Give us enough power and we will save you!" is the ready reply of government to a bewildered people crying, "Help us or we perish!"

Many of the framers of the American Constitution, like modern reformers, distrusted the ability of the masses to look after themselves. But they did not, for this reason, seek to make the state supreme. Quite the contrary. They knew only too well that government, once it becomes all-powerful, tends to be oppressive. Their compelling idea, therefore, was that government in the United States should be made the servant, the tool, the creature of the people. They were passionately determined to prevent the creation in America of personal rule or arbitrary government of any sort. They wished to master the government—not to be mastered by it. To this end they sought out ingenious devices to restrict men in authority. They set constitutional bounds on officials so as to make it hard for these men to exceed their allotted powers. They provided in the Constitution that certain rights of men were inalienable. Theirs was the concept of a government of laws which would be superior to whim and personal ambition—a government which would serve the people fairly—never coerce them arbitrarily.

Most governments have always been—and still are

today—of the master type. In fact, it may be generalized that arbitrary personal rule is the oldest kind of government—the type to which all governments most easily revert. The powers of the masters have, of course, been curtailed from time to time—as during the liberal movement of the seventeenth to nineteenth centuries. Out of this struggle came the few examples of government of the servant type—notably the pre-war government of the United States.

But let a crisis arise like a war or a great depression or a revolution, and at once, even in America, Constitution and laws are ignored and the ruler assumes full powers. He suspends the old forms and the old guarantees and denies the traditional rights of individuals—all, of course, in the name of the common good. Sometimes he acts without popular support, sometimes with the nation's full approval. In crises the people crave a leader, and readily grant him what he wants so long as they believe he will save them. Groping, baffled, uncertain, insecure, they seek certainty, security, light.

But crisis governments which have been useful during an emergency may menace the nation if the leaders try, when the crisis is past, to transform emergency measures and powers into permanent policies so as to strengthen their hold on the government. That this danger follows any great crisis is obvious for the human reason that men who have once tasted great power not only are reluctant to surrender it but easily come to look upon themselves as the only possible saviors of the nation. The greater their initial success the quicker their conviction that they are indispensable. And once a leader is sure that he is indispensable he easily persuades himself that he has a mission backed by the Almighty, and that it is thus his duty to stay in power indefinitely. Humility is rare in a politician riding the crest of the wave. History shows that too much power spoils the best of men. It is a heady drink, and easily intoxicates those who take it in ever larger draughts. Few indeed are the rulers who do not seek more power. Almost superhuman is he who resists the temptation to yield to whim, spite or malice— or to ill-humor and indigestion.

Too often leaders mistake their power for wisdom. They think that because they are strong, they must be wise; whereas their wisdom—if any—derives from within their own souls, the product of experience, knowledge and character. Occasionally such men are as wise as they would have the world think they are. A few—a very few—rule through some great inner light and strength. But to govern is for most men a heavy burden, however blithely they may shoulder it. When they lack the force of wisdom they fall back upon coercion. Usually the more a ruler resorts to compulsion the more he comes to depend on force in imposing his will. The greater the resistance he meets the more arbitrary he becomes. Opposition seems to him a form of insolence. Criticism is an affront to his intelligence, a reflection on his good intentions. His opponents, he is convinced, must be silenced if society is to be saved. If this cannot be done one way it must be done another.

Persons who have not had much contact with government officials do not realize how easy it is for such men to identify themselves with the offices which they hold. Too readily they confuse their own prejudices and desires with the powers and duties granted them by law and by the Constitution. In other words they look upon themselves as principals rather than as agents, as directors rather than as representatives, and it follows from this that their ideas acquire sanctity in their own sight, and their judgments and opinions seem to themselves infallible. Men in office are usually ignorant of the forces which they unleash, let alone those which they try to control. But they rarely underestimate their own capacities, and even though they may be stupid and foolish they neither know nor admit this.

The tragedy is that government, no matter how powerful, is no wiser than the men who govern. From the beginning of organized society rulers and philosophers have tried to devise means of enlisting talent and wisdom in government. But few indeed have been the occasions when wise and able men have served the state. Part of the trouble lies in the fact that wisdom and practical ability, rare by themselves, are even more rarely combined in the same person. Especially rare is the combination of wisdom about affairs of state with the ability to govern. The latter is the commoner quality, and can be developed by experience. The former is usually professed by teachers and philosophers, who, from Plato to John Dewey, have been notoriously incapable of applying their knowledge usefully in state affairs. Plato demonstrated the theory that a benevolent autocracy is the best kind of government. But not even Plato could show how a benevolent autocrat could be found. The various modern forms of state socialism, in so far as they rest on benevolent purposes, have much, in theory, to commend them. But they cannot function effectively except under the direction of men of true ability and wisdom. Nowhere do such men exist in abundance. A Mussolini is as rare as a Julius Cæsar. Hitler and Stalin have the dictator's technique, but lack benevolence. Most men in high office do not want big men about them. They prefer little men, yes-men, useful men, who will not make themselves objectionable by questioning the wisdom of the ruler's latest pet project.

What greater reflection is there on the stupidity of political leaders than the World War of 1914 and the so-called peace that came after it? Wise men would have prevented the war. Only blunderers could have framed such a travesty of peace as the pact of Versailles. Countless mistakes recorded in history were made because rulers lacked wisdom and knowledge. Power ignorantly used is one of the most destructive forces to which mankind can be subjected. The greater the power and the range of authority of the blunderer the greater the damage which he can do.

By the same token the greater the responsibility of the rulers—the more their duties are enlarged and the greater their control over highly complicated modern economic activities—the greater the need for wisdom and restraint on their part. It is not enough merely to wish to achieve desirable ends. It is not enough to assert that the state ought to undertake this and that function in the interest of the common good. The real problem is to discover some way of insuring that the bureaucrats who are to run the state-all-powerful, and the politicians who will choose them and supervise their activities, will know the complicated work which they are expected to perform, and will act wisely as well as benevolently.

A complex piece of industrial machinery, for example, operated by a man who does not understand it, is liable to destruction. A ship commanded by a captain and officers who are ignorant of its needs and capacities, do not agree as to its destination, and cannot plot its course, is sure to be shipwrecked. So government activities are not likely to be well performed by men who do not understand them and whose sole claim to office is their eagerness to eat out of the public trough.

In the face of these recorded facts the cry today nevertheless continues to be, "Give the state more power! Remove the checks on the executive and he will the more easily lead us out of the slough of despond!" The apparent belief of those who talk thus is that by enlarging the sphere of government and entrusting authority to an ever greater number of relatives and friends of the politicians in power, solutions will be found overnight for economic problems which have baffled men through the ages—problems many of which have their roots in the perversity of human nature.

Why believe that men who have had little or no experience except in petty personal enterprises can, by being named officials and clothed with wide powers, decide wisely how someone should carry on his business, of which they know nothing? When government turns to an expert on poultry-raising to formulate a gold currency policy why should the country expect a sound solution? Why think that a man who had been a failure as a journalist would make a success as an Ambassador, or that the heir to a sugar refinery would make a good Cabinet member?

Before considering the grant to government of even more powers than it now has it is well to examine just what the functions of government should be, and what its powers have been and now are.

Throughout history there have been swings from more to less control by government. But it may be generalized that, prior to the rise of political liberalism from the seventeenth through the nineteenth centuries, the privileges of the governing classes were almost unlimited and their attempted control covered all manner of economic as well as social activities. They included—at least at the height of the age of mercantilism—the fixing of prices, details as to the qualities of goods produced and often their amount, and even such things as the kind of clothes that could be worn and food that could be eaten.

From the age of Milton, Locke and Cromwell down to the middle of the nineteenth century the struggle to curtail privileges and to restrict the functions of government was increasingly successful. This took its form largely in efforts to impose constitutional and legal restrictions on the rulers. In America, where the battle was won earliest, it gained strength from the Jeffersonian doctrine that the best government is that which governs least. Largely under the influence of this theory men believed that government should be limited to the maintenance of order, the enforcement of law and justice, and the protection of the individual's rights and property.

But it was certain that to these bare functions of protection would soon be added services of one or other sort deemed in the common interest—the building and maintenance of public roads and canals, the transportation of the mails, the protection of public health and morals, etc. As this movement grew, the temptation to reformers to seek to use the machinery of government to impose their own standards of conduct on the country became irresistible. Eagerness to pry into and run the other fellow's personal affairs has always been an American characteristic. Uplifters, particularly if their cause can be presented as a high-sounding moral issue, glory in trying to make the neighbors do what the up-lifters believe they ought to do. Socially we are an intolerant people—and reformers, like revolutionists, thrive on intolerance. Theirs is the only sure road to sal-vation. If we refuse to be saved willingly it is the re-formers' duty to save us in spite of our apathy—or because of it.

This tendency to uplift the people by law reached its extreme in prohibition. The attempt to impose on the country at large the drinking prejudices of a little group of moral dyspeptics ran counter to all experience. Sump-tuary laws have been tried throughout the ages—and failed, for the obvious reason that you cannot, by law, make over the individual's preferences for food and drink. In Ancient Rome the reformers railed against the use of snow to cool beverages, and the fondness of rich Romans for shellfish. As Thomas S. Jerome once ob-served, many of these reformers sought to make a moral virtue of their own digestive insufficiency and attempted to deny to others those pleasures of the senses which they could themselves no longer enjoy.

Unfortunately the prohibition experiment strength-ened two bad American habits. The first, already referred to, is the tendency to use government as an agent of in-terference in other persons' affairs. The second—which grows out of the reaction against the first—is the readi-ness to ignore those laws which men do not like. Both are injurious to the common weal—the first because reform and uplift are relative matters involving conflicting interests and convictions which cannot be disposed of satisfactorily merely by imposing on the country the wishes of one little group by law; the second because whenever any particular law is flouted repeatedly and flagrantly, respect for all laws is weakened. Out of this grows not only a spirit of lawlessness but contempt for laws as rules of government, and a consequent readiness to lose respect for constituted authority.

When such respect is lost the very structure of society is in danger. No one questions the right to change the form of government. But thoughtful students of history are agreed that no government, be it good or bad, can last long when its citizens hold it in contempt. Good laws are, of course, the expression of organized society's will. But when laws are disregarded government itself is defied. Even though such defiance may be morally defensible on the ground that a particular law is a bad law, it is obvious that until that law, bad or good, is repealed, it must be enforced. The need is not for more laws but for more law enforcement. As William Graham Sumner facetiously put it a half century ago, the country would be better off if it could have a law to prevent bad lawmakers from passing any more bad laws.

The movement toward government interference did not, of course, stop with mere attempts to reform morals. As the abuses incidental to the greed of men intent on piling up great wealth in a new country became more acute, government sought to restrain unwholesome economic activities. Beginning with efforts to check corruption and unfair practices, it attacked monopolies and price fixing and then gradually extended its powers of regulation over many kinds of business activities. Transportation and finance early came under its supervision. In recent years almost every branch of business and farming has been directly or indirectly affected by the laws and activities of the Federal government. The government is now engaged in banking, insurance, and the manufacture and distribution of electric power. It dispenses billions of dollars in doles, relief and financial aid. It controls farm production and restricts industrial operations.

Prior to the World War the functions of government could still be summarized as three-fold: (1) to maintain order, law and justice; (2) to perform services for the community which the citizens cannot well perform for themselves; and, (3) to check abuses in the economic activities of the country. Today at least two more functions are being added: (4) to plan for the nation's economic development over a period of years, and, (5) to devise means of forcing the people to carry out the wishes of the party in power. In other words, government is once more making itself all-powerful.

Thus is the cycle of reaction nearing completion. In America as elsewhere government is resuming functions of which it was stripped two centuries ago. For those in office this is splendid. They realize that not only is authority being restored to them with the sanction of the governed, but that new opportunities—undreamed-of opportunities—to entrench themselves and their friends in power, perhaps permanently, are now theirs for the grasping. As more new functions are surrendered to the politicians their disregard of restraint increases. The more authority government wields the less it has to pause to consider personal rights. Aristotle foresaw correctly twenty-four centuries ago that the abuses and weaknesses of democracy lead apparently inevitably to a form of autocracy.

III

THE ART OF POLITICS

IF GOVERNMENT is to be all-powerful it is proper to ask: Who are to be the governors?

In historic times government has been in the hands of politicians. Theoretically, therefore, politics should be the science of government. In fact, politics is the art of getting and holding public office. When there were personal monarchies, this involved the activities and intrigues of the courtier. In popular governments it requires the traditional methods of the demagogue. The rules are as old as organized society. They have been written about voluminously since the days of Plato and Aristotle but have changed surprisingly little.

If a modern Lord Chesterfield were to give advice to his son embarking on a political career he would doubtless speak somewhat as follows:

Your success will depend largely on your ability to smile and to promise everything to everyone. Learn, therefore, to be a good handshaker and mixer and to kiss the babies. Agree with everyone about everything. Do not forget that most men are more interested in your promises than in your achievements. They want to believe that you are their friend—that you want to do the

right thing by them. Never miss a chance, therefore, to
make plain your eagerness to improve the individual lot
of the underprivileged. Promise them everything they
want and, if you are really wise, try to do for them some
of the things they desire most. Your efforts will convince
them of your good will. This will make them your friends,
and they will repay your friendship by voting for you.

Do not make the mistake of trying to be consistent.
Your living will depend on your continuation in office.
If you cannot stay in power one way, change your course.
If a cause which you have espoused is losing its popular
appeal attach yourself to another which promises more
votes. Votes, after all, are what get you and keep you in
office, so do nothing that can lose votes and do everything that may win them for you. Votes mean, in the final
analysis, numbers. What you need is as many votes as
possible. Do not look for numbers among the educated
and the wealthy. They are few—very few. Look, rather,
to the masses. Advocate anything which may be popular
with them. Ingratiate yourself with them. Assure them
that they are not getting their due, and repeat, over and
over again, that you will help them.

When it comes to a campaign, begin by maligning
your opponent in well-chosen private conversations.
Denounce his acts in public and attack his motives. If
possible, dig up some discreditable incident in his private
life. Do not be too particular about the truth of what
you charge, but be sure you paint a rosy picture while

you are about it. Remember that a denial or correction never catches up with the original slander, and that it flatters many men to hear evil of their leaders.

If you are in doubt about issues, follow Aristotle's admonition that it is always safe to denounce the rich as the source of all troubles, and to charge that your opponent is the tool of the rich. Make plain your eagerness to see wealth more evenly distributed. Side with the debtors against the creditors. Set the masses against the classes, and proclaim yourself the champion of the oppressed. Promise that the government will do more and more for the poor, but insist that the costs must and will be borne by the rich. Never admit that you will increase any taxes except those that you can pin on the wealthy. Advocate every reform that has any chance of proving popular, and do not feel under any obligation to carry it out if you are elected. You can always count on the short memory of the public.

When one of your policies fails to work or becomes unpopular, divest yourself of responsibility for it, blame your opponents for its failure, and at once advocate something new. The voters want change and distraction. Hence do not hesitate to resort frequently to pulling white rabbits out of high hats. A diversion is always useful—even when everything is apparently going well. You are, after all, an actor on the public stage, and the public soon tires even of a favorite who plays a monotonous role. Variety is the spice of public life.

If you make a blunder, never admit it. Blame one of your subordinates and, if necessary, discharge him publicly for the mistake which you yourself made. He probably will not dare "tell on you," and even if he does, he will be believed only by those who are already your opponents. If this sacrifice of a scapegoat fails to appease the public and the situation becomes embarrassing, at once propose a new plan for helping the multitude. This will prove your benevolence—that you want to do the right thing by the people.

Under no circumstances tie yourself irrevocably to any particular course of action. Remember that if you are to hold office, you must be prepared to run with the hare and hunt with the hounds. You are, to use another simile, like the quarterback on a football team, and must be ready to change your play in accordance with the progress of the game. Leave "causes" and reforms to uplifters and other fanatics, until you are sure that they will be popular. Then embrace them—but never too tightly. It is your job to be always just a little ahead of public opinion, and public opinion changes quickly. But under no circumstances get too far ahead. The people are not interested in the future—only in today.

In your speeches, do not be specific. The voters like generalities—especially if they are phrased in fine-sounding, benevolent terms. Avoid facts. They may be used against you by your enemies. If, however, it is necessary to give an appearance of definiteness, do not be squeamish about mere accuracy. Make a positive statement, with figures to support your case, even if neither the facts nor the figures are as you say they are. Only a few people will check on you, and by the time your opponents have discovered your deception and have tried to pillory you publicly for misrepresentation, the people will have lost interest. If not, you can make another speech to divert them.

In these days of radio, it is not what you say, but how you say it, that counts. Few people will ever read your speeches, but millions will listen to you on the air. Therefore, cultivate a mellifluous voice. Study phrasing and emphasis. Make your tones as rich and variable as possible and, above all, speak with ringing conviction and transparent sincerity. The voters will believe you if you talk as if you yourself believe what you say. Your intonation will convince them even more than the things that you promise.

In such a strain our modern Chesterfield might continue indefinitely. The son would soon learn from experience that in the conduct of practical politics there is necessarily much back-scratching. In a government based on popular elections, a man can get ahead in politics only if he is prepared to help those who can help him. Hence there are combinations and deals—sometimes sinister and crooked, more often practical agreements to work together for different ends. The politician who fails to do favors for his constituents is in danger of being defeated when he comes up for reelection or advancement. One who refuses to help his political associates gets little help from them in return and so finds it hard to accomplish anything.

The truly successful politician is a master at finding jobs for his supporters. These need not be government positions, but it goes without saying that the more government jobs at his disposal the better. Many government jobs are easy and, if the party remains in power, have a long life.

The next best thing to giving potential supporters jobs is to give them financial assistance. Men and women who depend on government aid are sure to show that type of gratitude which has been defined as a lively sense of benefits to come. It is a safe axiom, therefore, that if government can spend money freely—even if only on a dole—it can fasten to itself with hoops of depreciated currency a large army of sure supporters. It stands to reason that in a political system in which numbers control—*i.e.*, in which ballots are honestly counted—there are great advantages in having a large body of dependent—and dependable—voters. These should, if possible, be made secure in those precincts and wards in the cities which dominate the pivotal electoral districts. By a judicious study of past election returns, it is easy to determine where votes are most needed. There most relief money should be spent.

Reformers and uplifters seem not to realize that even a long-entrenched political boss holds his position in the political machine only tenuously. Only a small—a very small—fraction of one percent of the voters of the country actually runs the machinery of the two major political parties. It follows, therefore, that a really determined little group can, if it will work as hard and consistently as the professional politicians, easily succeed in boring from within and seizing control of the machine. True, custom and law have given those now in control of the political parties a tight grip on the machines from the election districts up. They cannot be dislodged by merely calling for new blood and new faces in the party management. Practical politics is their livelihood and usually the pride of their hearts, and they cling to their powers as barnacles to a ship's bottom. Often they can show long records of real services to countless individuals in their community—little services, most of them, but the kind of services that mean much in social and political relations. But if a group of aggressively determined citizens is willing to attend the local party meetings consistently, to organize its own followers in each election district, and to see to it that these followers continue to take an active part in local affairs, it can with comparative ease bring about a change in party control and effect party reforms. The strength of the machine leaders is their organization. The lesson of Lenin in Russia is that the machinery of politics can be taken over readily by a group that is even more closely knit and better organized than the one in power.

Unfortunately time and persistence are indispensable to the winning of the control of a political machine, and most reformers of the more polite sort lack both. Hence party dominance remains by default in the hands of the ward politicians—and party dominance involves the nominating of the party candidates and hence control of the party's—and probably ultimately the nation's—policies.

Rich malefactors have, of course, used this system to their advantage. But such influence as they still possess over politicians is theirs largely because those who would deprive them of their power and would "clean up" politics are too lazy and indifferent to put up a prolonged fight. They are week-end reformers—willing to spend an hour on Sunday denouncing the sins of politicians, but devoting the rest of the week to their own affairs. Professional politicians do not even do these critics the honor of hating them. They feel only contempt—the contempt of the doer for the talker, of the experienced chauffeur for the back-seat driver.

It is no solution for disgusted citizens to adopt the role of Pontius Pilate and wash their hands of the matter. Professional politicians are as they are because the public is apathetic. The ethics of politicians are not necessarily worse than those of other men. Rather is their occupation such that they cannot be too strict about their standards. Political life demands a rubber conscience. Even the most upright man, once elected to office, finds himself faced with the major dilemma—whether to do what the majority of his constituents think they want done, or what he himself believes should be done. This choice involves, in the final analysis, two conflicting philosophies of representative government. According to one, the elected official is merely the mouthpiece for his electorate, bound by their restrictions and wishes. According to the other, he is an independent agent, elected in order to use his own judgment and ability as best he may in the interest of his constituents. According to the former philosophy, he is the follower, according to the latter, the leader, of public opinion.

Recently, as will be more amply developed in a later chapter, a third doctrine has received wide support—that the head of the party in office receives, when he is elected, a "mandate" to do whatsoever he wishes, and that it is the duty of his party members to follow his leadership without question. In other words, lesser elected officials—Congressmen, for example—are to disregard not only the known wishes of their constituents but also their own best judgment and are to perform the bidding of the head of the state, in the name of the popular mandate which he has received. This technique has been most successfully followed by Mr. Hitler in Germany.

Where such divergent moral choices await those who

seek public office, it is clear that politics is not an easy career. In fairness to most politicians, it must be said that, barring everything touching on their election or reelection to office, they try to do what they believe is right. It is only when campaigns approach or when, as in the case of many of the highest national officers, like Senators or the President, they must be continually thinking of reelection, that they follow the traditional pattern of the professional office-seeker and office-holder, outlined at the beginning of this chapter. As a former Governor of a New England state who for twenty years was a successful popular leader recently put it, continued office-holding saps a man's integrity of character. He is too much taken up with doing things which he knows should not be done and with saying things which he does not believe. This is unavoidable if politics is his lifework, for his object must always be to remain in office. Usually, defeat means not only the loss of power and prestige but a downward step in the economic scale.

Take, for example, a Congressman from almost any district. So long as he is in office, he is one of the leaders of his community. His wife and children enjoy social honors. They spend a part of each year in Washington, where not only he is helping to run the country but where, from the point of view of his friends and neighbors, he is in contact with the great of the land. The President—if he is of the same party—is his friend. If of another party, the President—so the Congressman's followers are sure to believe—fears and respects him. Furthermore, he makes $10,000 a year plus an allowance for a secretary and a messenger, who are often relatives of his, free franking privileges, travel allowances and other perquisites—an income which for most members of Congress is far beyond their greatest expectations in private life. So long as he can be reelected, therefore—or sent to the Senate—he is on the top of the world. If he is defeated, he returns home with prestige shaken and with the stultifying "ex" before his former title—a formal badge that he is now a has-been. No longer is he "our Congressman." He is merely an unsuccessful politician out of a job—and out of an income of about $15,000 a year. His wife, instead of being somebody of importance, able to spend the winters in Washington, with side trips to Florida, returns to the local sewing circle and her own housework, no longer flattered by those who, in reality, envied her her good fortune and were convinced that their husbands would have served the community better in Congress than hers.

Is it surprising that, under such circumstances, the average politician trims his sails to what he believes to be the popular course—that he compromises with his conscience if his conscience urges action which might prevent his reelection? Politicians are, after all, merely human—usually, incidentally, warmly human and intuitive. Their livelihood demands that they be friendly, helpful and loyal. Much of their time is spent in doing things for others. They have been well called "social workers not interested in reform." Necessarily they are more concerned with people than with principles, because their life work is given over to contacts with people of all kinds—usually people who want their help, or whose votes the politicians need. Few men have ever been successful in politics who have not possessed in a high degree the art of making friends. Friends are the politicians' ladder to success. If a politician has to choose between sacrificing a friend and sacrificing a principle, he rarely hesitates to give up the latter. If, as is usually the case, he is a ready promiser, this also is because of his unwillingness to alienate actual and potential friends. He wants to do what he can for everyone. If he fails, it is not through lack of good will but because of events beyond his control. Incidentally the demands on him for help of all kinds are far in excess of the demands on the average mortal, and he has to give of his time and power unsparingly. He retains his place only so long as he remains active. Hence, for him, politics is an endless adventure—not one to be pursued intermittently or as a side-line.

It is the merit of the average politician that he is truly representative of his people. He knows them and their wants and weaknesses. He is in constant touch with them. From this it is a natural corollary that his horizon is largely limited by their interests. Local problems are more important to him than national issues because the

local problems are of concern to his people. His livelihood and his continuation in power rest on his ability
to help his people—to make them realize that he has
their interests, in fact, at heart. Hence he necessarily is
guided by what he believes will be popular rather
than by what he thinks is right—provided he happens
to pay much, if any, attention to what is right or
wrong.

Unfortunately those qualities which make a successful
ward politician do not prepare a man for great national
leadership. The larger the scale of the politician's activities, the greater his need for a grasp of large problems.
But in practice this grasp is rarely his, for the simple
reason that the average politician who has reached high
national office is little more than a slightly magnified
successful ward leader. He carries into national fields
the same dominant ambition to obtain votes and to hold
office. Hence his interest is necessarily more in what is
popular than in what is of national concern—in what
will induce his constituents to reelect him rather than in
what may seem to promise to advance the national interest in the distant future. Necessarily the politician is a
man of the hour. His concern is with things of the present—the demands of his constituents, the needs of the
campaign, the interests of his party. The future—even
four years away—is unimportant except in so far as it
may affect his reelection, and he knows that many things
may happen within a year or two or three. Therefore,

he not only never crosses a bridge before he comes to it but he pays little attention to bridges of any kind until they are under his feet.

It has often been observed by Lord Bryce and others that public opinion is a check on the activities of politicians. This is—or rather was—true. But today the politicians are learning how to control public opinion. In Europe governments dominate all radio broadcasting. In this country, broadcasting, though in the hands of privately owned broadcasting stations, is subject to constant checks by the government. The operation of a station is very costly—and as licenses to operate must be obtained from the Federal Communications Commission, and are good for only six months (subject to renewal at the pleasure of the government), the stations take pains to see that nothing goes on the air which might induce the F.C.C. to deny a renewal of a license. What this means, in practice, is that, while the spokesmen of the political party in power, and, in particular, the President himself, can use the radio whenever and as much as desired, the air is not as accessible to the administration's critics. During national campaigns the big chains have tried to allot time to both parties more or less evenly. But the fact remains that they fear the administration in power and the administration has all the advantages of the "ins" versus the "outs," regardless of party affiliations.

The Federal government has not been slow in apply-

ing modern publicity and advertising methods to the
stimulation of favorable public opinion. In recent years
hundreds of skilled publicity agents have been employed
by various bureaus in Washington, charged with delug-
ing the press and the public with propaganda favorable
to the administration's activities. The avowed purpose
is "educational." The real object is, however, to try to
capture votes at the next election by building up good
will for the administration.

In Europe the attempts of those in power to control
public opinion have not stopped with domination of the
radio. The press almost everywhere on the continent is
subject to censorship or punishment. Even in Great
Britain, editors receive "suggestions" from the government that criticism of certain major actions be post-
poned in times of crises, or that certain acts be favorably
explained. On the continent, the mail of known or sus-
pected critics and enemies of the government is watched
and often their movements and conversations are spied
upon. When they show signs of becoming troublesome,
they are either exiled, imprisoned or murdered.

In America, as yet, little more has been done than to
attempt to "get something" on the administration's
critics. Whether or not the income tax bureau has been
used to this end, the fact that many critics of the
administration have believed that it is being so used has
deterred the more timid among them from asserting
themselves.

Every President in the last thirty years has had his own way of influencing the press—some by personal blandishments lavished upon the owners of newspapers, others by particular attention to Washington correspondents. It would be wrong to charge that such attempts have been improper. A President not only has the right but the duty to see that his acts and intentions are given full and fair publicity. But the result has been that the administration in power is able to exercise an influence over the news which, while not so great as its power over the radio, has been distinctly advantageous to the "ins."

The danger lies in the readiness of men in power to resort to extremes. Hostile criticism is all the more bitter to a President in proportion to his conviction that he is trying to do the right thing. He knows that much of the criticism is captious and has as its sole purpose discrediting him for reelection. He is naturally reluctant to admit the same degree of sincerity in his opponents as among his friends. Hence he is always tempted to try in one or other way to silence his critics. Since Presidents have had the example of European authoritarian states before them and their own followers keep dinning in their ears that their critics are the enemies of the nation as well as of the administration, and may make reforms impossible of achievement, small wonder that Presidents seek some subtle way of suppressing all who differ from them.

The marvel is that, with the politicians' compelling need to play politics, so much government work is fairly adequately carried out. As a rule it is costly. Usually it is cumbersome and delayed by red tape. Often it is unnecessary and foolish. But certain services continue to be performed by government—and well performed, despite the pressure on the politicians to think more of reelection than of the job in hand.

. . . .

If it be objected that much of what has been said above does not apply to bureaucrats under the civil service, the answer is that bureaucracy has its own defects. It can be, like the English or Dutch civil service, capable and energetic. More often than not, it is impeccably honest. But bureaucracy has two great vices—it becomes hopelessly involved in red tape, and it is never satisfied to stay within its allotted bounds. When men are put on the government payroll, they are initiated first into the mysteries of endless blank forms. Next they learn how to avoid doing anything that can be embarrassing for themselves or their superiors. Then they take refuge in routine, which knows no time—only channels and initials. It is much more important to those who are the slaves of routine that a matter be properly put on paper, referred through proper channels to the proper persons, and initialed by those individuals before being once more put in motion, than that it receive prompt action. In fact, one of the principal maxims of all bureaucracies is, "When in doubt, delay." Long experience has shown that delay has a way of making it unnecessary to solve many questions—and the solution of questions involves possible responsibility which, in turn, implies potential punishment. It is usual in a bureaucracy for the underling who makes the mistake to receive the blame, but for the chief to take all credit for any good work done by his assistants. Hence responsibility is to be avoided like the plague.

The other vice—that of expansionism—has wrecked many governments. The larger the number of persons on the public payroll the greater the need for increasing the government's revenues. Hence the larger the bureaucracy the higher the taxes which the government has to impose. Each government department likes to add to its jurisdiction. This means, of course, to enlarge its personnel. The bureau chiefs and department heads welcome this, as it means more power for them, and most men in public life—even in the bureaucracies—enjoy exercising power. Bit by bit new agencies are added—and new millions of dollars to the payroll.

In this expansion politicians are usually as interested as the bureaucrats—especially if they can arrange to have the new posts filled without regard to civil service requirements. Jobs are always dear to the politicians' hearts—and so is government spending. Both enable the men in office to add their relatives and friends in ever-increasing numbers to the public payroll. This is a great advantage to them, as each such appointee is supposed to be able to influence the votes of his family and a few friends, and so to add to the strength of the party in power. This is why hardly any public office—including that of local foreman in the C.C.C. camps—is open to any one who does not have the endorsement of his local political leaders—of the party in power. In the old days they called this the "spoils system." Today, it is euphoniously termed "filling non-career posts." In Europe, before the depression, it had become almost a fine art. Men of all classes aspired to a place on the government payroll—not only because it gave them power, prestige and a sure income, but because the state was an easy taskmaster.

One of the greatest mistakes the founders of the American government made was in assuming that government service would attract only the best men. True, their mistake is understandable in view of the unusually high calibre of the members of the Constitutional Convention, and many of the state and Federal officials prior to Jackson's day. But in time the levelling effect of democracy lowered the calibre of all public servants, with the result that the word "politician" became a term of reproach. We are as far today as ever from Plato's ideal of a government of the best—and never has the world had greater need of good and wise men in government.

IV

PROPERTY, BASIS OF FREEDOM

THE OWNERS of property have usually controlled the
state. When, as in Europe before the French Revolution,
property was in the hands of an aristocracy, the government also was in its hands. When, as in the United States
in the first half of the nineteenth century, the ownership
of property was widely distributed among the people, a
truly popular form of government existed. Two generations later, when great banking and industrial fortunes
were concentrated in the hands of a comparatively few
men, political control became theirs. Wealth and political
power seem to go together, as if by some sort of natural
law. This is as true among primitive peoples as in the
United States, Great Britain or other Western countries.
The rich have always been influential.

The cause of this phenomenon concerns us less than
its social and political implications. Radicals and con-
servatives agree in deploring the trend toward government of the very rich, for the very rich and by the minions of the very rich. Where they part company is in their
cure for this admitted social evil. Modern radical thought
inclines toward the socialization of wealth and property.
Liberals, in contrast, believe that the holding of

property must be decentralized—that property must be restored to as large a portion of the population as possible.

Here are two opposing theories. The one wishes to abolish private property. The other wishes to spread the ownership of private property among as many families as possible. The one places the emphasis on a collectivist entity called society. The other believes that men and women are more important than the state—that what ministers to their personal well-being should, if possible, be placed within their grasp. The one, contemptuous of the average man's ability to fend for himself, wishes to protect him and direct him. The other, aware that self-reliance and self-help are indispensable to the spiritual as well as the economic development of man, seeks to help as many as possible to attain this objective.

The advocates of the redistribution of property are convinced that society still rests on the family and that the family still centers around the hearth—even if this be only a gas range or a radiator. They know that economic and spiritual values attach to the ownership of a home. No trailer, no tenement, no rented farm, can ever mean as much as the home that is owned. Better a shack on a lot that belongs than a palace for which rent is paid. Ownership of a home stimulates all the constructive forces in man's moral nature. It furnishes the roots without which no family can attain its full spiritual development. It supplies a form of financial and mental security that no mere rented house can ever give. When a family ceases to own the home it lives in, when it no longer has a plot of land, however small, where a few vegetables and flowers can be grown, when its members are no longer attached to a bit of soil that they can call their own, it is on the verge of social degradation. The propertyless throughout the ages have been the depressed —and the oppressed. They have ever been at the mercy of the rich and powerful.

Conversely, men of property have been free. The ownership of property has implied, from the earliest days, a degree of economic independence. In the history of Europe those who did not own land were little more than slaves—always excepting the craftsmen and merchants of the towns. Property was a means to an independent livelihood. He who owned land was freed from the necessity of working for someone else. The ownership of land thus early became identified with personal freedom. In fact the term "freeman" long applied only to men of property. They had more rights and powers than the propertyless—and more responsibilities. Having a stake in the country they were naturally the preservers of order, the conservators of traditions, the upholders of law, the "sound men" of the community. In contrast, families without property, men and women without a stake in the land, those who are mere subsistence wage-earners or sub-marginal tenants, never have had, and cannot be expected to have, the same interest in the community as the propertied classes. They feel that they have little to risk in any change in the economic and political order. Hence they can easily be persuaded that they will gain much by a new deal of the social cards. They are the dispossessed, the army of the have-nots, readily mobilized by demagogues against the haves.

Because of the great inequalities in property holding and because of the advantages which those with large property have over those with little or none, many reformers believe that the tendency for the large to become larger and the small smaller is irresistible. It will be irresistible, of course, if everyone accepts it without a struggle. But past concentrations of great wealth have been broken up. In France, the large estates were partitioned as a result of the revolution of 1789. Small landholders have predominated there for a century and a half. In Denmark, seventy years ago, nearly half the farm land was operated by tenants. Today, only seven percent of it is so operated. Denmark has become a nation of small landowners. In Ireland recent laws have facilitated the partition of the estates through government intervention, and the establishment of many families on small plots. Even in America, the Federal government has helped to finance the acquisition of farms and homes. No more valuable social work has been attempted in many years. But much still remains to be done in devising methods of helping competent tenants to acquire farms and homes. Above all, a premium must be put upon ownership instead of, as at present, taxing it so highly that only the well-to-do can afford to own property.

There has been talk of "abolishing" private property. Not private property as an institution, but the abuses of private property, require attention and correction. The institution is too deeply ingrained in human experience to be eradicable. The abuses—the concentration of too much property, the unwillingness of owners to use property productively, the sterilization of property through excessive taxation—these and similar problems need the most careful thought and study. But they should be approached with the idea in mind that what is necessary is to distribute property more widely, and that ownership of property should be insured and facilitated by government, instead of being penalized. Nothing is gained by mere "spite" reforms—by advocating proposed solutions which will merely "soak the rich" and punish the successful.

It is, of course, true that in an era of unrestrained individualism such as America knew from the Civil War down to the great depression, everything facilitated the concentration of wealth and ownership. But this tendency has existed just as much in other ages and countries. It is not an exclusive manifestation of the industrial age. It was one of the causes of the downfall of the Roman Empire. It helped produce the French Revolution. It is one of the evils directly traceable to greed, cupidity and avarice on the one hand, and docility, stupidity and credulity on the other. It has its origin not in a particular form of society such as "capitalism," but in the perversity of human nature. Aristotle, in criticizing Plato's proposal for the communal holding of property, warned that "men readily listen to it, and are easily induced to believe that in some wonderful manner, everybody will become everybody's friend, especially when some one is heard denouncing the evils now existing in states, suits about contracts, convictions for perjury, flatteries of rich men and the like, which are said to arise out of the possession of private property." He added knowingly that "these evils, however, are due to a very different cause—the wickedness of human nature."

If there is to be a proper understanding of the problem of the restoration of property, it is essential to get rid of the false ideas about property and ownership that have been spread by collectivists for several generations. The origin of property is as old as the adjective "mine"—and the adjective is as old as the race. Even a dog is possessive and resents efforts of other dogs to take away a toy or a bone or to occupy a favorite chair or cushion. Children from an early age show a sense of ownership. While this is in part in response to suggestion and example, it is also instinctive, for without possession and self-assertion there is little chance of survival.

Beginning with food, clothing, and implements, property early expanded to include hunting rights and ranges, animals and, finally, fields. While pastures and hunting ranges were occasionally held as communal property, there are no authoritative records of any agricultural or industrial civilization in which productive land was held and worked communally. Some of the church lands in the Middle Ages were farmed for the benefit of the monastic orders and their dependents. But, by and large, ownership was predominantly in the hands of the landlords, held and transmitted in the family so that the property would remain intact.

Until comparatively modern times, real property and wealth were virtually synonymous, as valuable property consisted almost exclusively of land and buildings. With the development of financial and industrial enterprises in the nineteenth century, property came to embrace shares of stock and other accumulations of capital. Whereas in the old days great fortunes were almost exclusively invested in land, today land forms but a part of most fortunes. Land retains, nevertheless, its enormous social value for the simple reason that society cannot exist without land, and that the wider the distribution of the ownership of land, the firmer the foundations of the state.

Those who maintain that all property once was communally owned rest their case on the false assumption that land, like air or water, is a "gift of nature," and that no man has any more right to own a given plot of land than a fixed body of air. Reasoning from the fact that numerous pastoral and hunting tribes have held lands in common for the tribe, they assumed that private property had its origin in selfish seizure of communal property by aggressive individuals.

While there have been robbers in all ages, this is a parody of the history of the origin of personal property. Ownership of a given piece of property was inseparable from the spread of agriculture. Primitive men, like their civilized descendants, were reluctant to go to all the labor of clearing, digging, planting and cultivating a field if other people were to have the harvest. Hence from the beginning of settled agricultural communities, the secure private ownership of land became a matter of vital importance to society. Landowners became the pillars of ordered society, the props of government. In fact, it is no exaggeration to generalize that civilization grew in direct proportion to the security of private property. When property was insecure, civilization languished or retrogressed. When it was properly protected, civilization advanced. Property was the basis of all capital, and so of all the improvements due to a capitalistic society. When a man cleared a piece of earth, improved it and planted it, he indulged in that form of foresight and self-denial which is fundamental in the formation of capital. Without thrift, saving, forethought and self-denial, there would have been little progress in the world.

The man who plants an orchard or an olive tree plans and looks ahead. He goes without the use of the crops from the land so planted during the years that the trees are maturing. Thus he creates capital. Thereafter, so long as he tills his soil and tends his trees, they give him an income out of which, if he continues to be prudent, he will save a part and either re-invest it in the soil by adding fertilizer, or perhaps extend the area of his orchard. The improvements which he puts into his land are so much added capital. They have been made possible by his willingness to save, to plan and to work hard.

To this extent, the ownership of property is a stimulus to economic development. But this, as already pointed out, is only one of the values of ownership. Self-subsistence, while vitally important, is no more so than the opportunities for the full development of personal and family life through self-dependence. Much has been written—by city folks—about the troubles of farmers. But hard as is life on farms in many parts of America, it has its compensations which no mere wage-slavery in a factory town can ever give. The farmer has his ups and downs, his fat and lean years. He is at the mercy of the weather. He is driven to labor hard and long. His life is often lonely. But he is not liable to sudden unemployment, and to find himself without house, food and clothing, forced to beg for charity or receive a dole.

Obviously all men cannot—and many men would not —be farmers. But there are millions who would be happier if they could own a house and a few acres, even though their employment might continue to be in industry. There are other millions who would be happier owning their own homes in cities, towns and villages. Both these groups need encouragement and help. They are the ones to whom restoration of property would mean most.

It is one thing to enable a man to acquire property. It is something quite different to be sure that he and his family will continue to hold it. Certainly he will not do so if he is not eager to hold it, and ready to make the necessary sacrifices of work to hold it. Property has always been, to a certain extent, a measure of personal energy and ability. The man who is willing to work hard and to deny himself present indulgences for future benefits has rarely found it impossible to acquire property in America. Such men were acquiring—and retaining— property even in the worst of the depression. But the man who lacks initiative, or who is lazy, or who believes that society owes him a living, will not be able to hold the property that has been given him. He is the type that William Graham Sumner described as believing that because there are those who have been prudent for themselves, they should be forced to be prudent for others. His type believes that—again I quote from Sumner—"if a man wants anything which he has not got it is the fault of somebody else who ought to be found and compelled to give it to him."

Such men will, of course, never acquire property— except by pillage, theft or government dispensation.

But they form a comparatively small part of the population. It must not be forgotten that freedom to own, to acquire property, was one of the compelling motives that drove men to emigrate from Europe to America. They sought economic independence through property, and most of them hoped to make enough to relieve their children of the hardships that they themselves underwent when they were young. Incidentally, it is not inconceivable that the very large measure of their success is partly responsible for the apparent lack of appreciation of the social as well as the personal value of property shown by their children. For too many of the younger generation property was too easily come by. Hence they did not value it. But unless the forces of demoralization increase with great rapidity we shall continue to have in this country a large body of persons to whom the ideal of owning a home or a farm or a business is still worth struggling for.

Compared to England the United States is by no means in a hopeless situation with respect to ownership. True, 42 percent of the farms in America are operated by tenants, but when account is taken of those who are already working to acquire the farms they operate, and of those who lease farms from relatives and will later inherit them, it may be said that two-thirds of the farmers in the country are actual or intended owners. To be sure, this proportion is much smaller than seventy years ago. But it has been compensated in part by the increase in the number of persons in towns and cities who live in houses which they own. This percentage has grown, for example, from 34.7 in 1900 to 45.7 in 1930. In many of the Northern cities in particular the growth has been steady and encouraging.

So also, while there has been a rapid increase in the spread of chain stores and mail order retail businesses in recent years, about four-fifths of the retail business in America is still carried on by individual merchants who are their own bosses and who employ only a handful of "help" apiece. In industry, of course, while there are still many privately owned small factories, the great bulk of the volume is produced by the big corporations.

Even though these figures compare favorably with other countries, there is no denying the fact that ownership in America is on the decline and the number of men engaged in business for themselves is decreasing. Conversely the number of homeless wage-earners is increasing. Hence more heads of families are losing their independence, and are at the mercy of corporate employers who may deprive them of their jobs without notice. This means, in the long run, the change of the social composition of the nation from one in which most men work for themselves and have their own homes, to one in which they work for others and live in others' houses.

That this is social retrogression no thoughtful person can doubt. It contains the seeds of national demoralization. It will end by destroying democracy and liberty.

Wages and rent mean, inevitably, dependence. The larger the number of the propertyless and the larger the fortunes of the rich, the easier it is for the rich to dominate the state and use it for their own short-sighted, selfish ends. The restoration of property means, *per contra,* the increase of the sound political influence of the small farmers, small merchants and professional men, thus curbing the power of the industrial and financial magnates. At the same time the increase of the number of property holders means the increase of the number of persons possessing a measure of economic freedom.

That a successful program of restoring property would eliminate the "depressed third" is improbable. There is in this as in every other country a substantial part of the population which cannot or will not take care of itself. The truth is that poverty has been the normal lot of most of mankind from the very beginning of the human race. Those individuals and occasional groups that have raised themselves above poverty have kept above it only with great difficulty. The least inattention or carelessness, the least laziness or indifference, a stroke of bad luck, and even men of large fortunes have returned to the dead level of poverty.

Except through property and work there is no escape from poverty. The pioneers knew this. Hence they worked to acquire property. They sensed the fact that property was security, and they knew that those who could work and refused to do so were parasites. This explains their constant emphasis on the necessity to work. This also explains their dread of "going on the county," which to them implied failure, laziness and shiftlessness. If this also led them into the error of assuming that all who failed materially in life did so because of sin and vice, it may be blamed on confusing theology with economics. No more un-Christian doctrine was ever expounded than that an entire class of people is condemned to poverty through its spiritual and moral defects, and that wealth is a badge of merit.

In the final analysis, all comes back to personal effort. There is a vast difference between helping people to help themselves, and merely doing something to help them. So long as the objective is spiritual and economic independence, men must be encouraged to work, to save and to own. In other words, everything possible must be done to enable the propertyless to acquire homes, and wage-earners to become their own bosses. Government can help, but it cannot compel. Now as always, self-reliance, industry and self-control are the determining factors. To the extent that men are unequal in capacities and fortune, there will be inequalities in their acquisition of property. To the ambitious and the self-reliant, property has always been a stimulant. So it will continue to be unless collectivists succeed in socializing private property, and thus at one stroke deprive the most constructive, productive portion of mankind of its incentive to work, and even to exist.

V

PRODUCTION, KEY TO PROSPERITY

INCREASED production at cheaper costs is the key to many pressing problems. The world needs more goods—more food, more houses, more conveniences, more comforts. Only if these can be produced in sufficient quantity and at sufficiently low prices can more people be enabled to enjoy more of the material good things of life. The multiplication of those goods which men want and need is indispensable if the "under-privileged" are to be helped. In the multiplication of these goods more men and women will find work. By the multiplication of these goods, many of the economic inequalities between men will be ironed out. New production means new wealth, and new wealth must be created before it can be shared.

It is true, of course, that sharing the wealth may be accomplished by division, instead of by multiplication. But any share-the-wealth movement which is based on dividing up the present fortunes of the rich among the poor will ruin the former without enriching the latter, for the simple reason that there are not enough goods in existence today to satisfy the needs or wants of the have-nots. In contrast, a share-the-wealth movement which has as its underlying purpose the creation of as

much new wealth as possible and its partition among as
many people as possible, is sure to be beneficial.

In the final analysis wealth is not money but things—
the things which men use to live. Before the nineteenth
century wealth consisted largely of goods made by hand
out of the products of agriculture and forestry. Today,
new wealth is the result primarily of mechanical power
applied to metals. Ours is not only a machine age but a
mineral age. Every radio, every automobile, every tin
can, bears witness to our reliance on metals and processes
which were unfamiliar to our great-grandfathers. Structural steel is a modern product. Aluminum was little
used before the World War. Copper had only restricted
uses before electricity was widely developed a generation
ago.

So completely mechanized has our civilization become
that we tend to forget how recent is the discovery and
development of our common types of motive power. Before 1800 the work of the world was done by men, reinforced only by horses and oxen. Here and there the wind
was harnessed, or small streams. But steam as a source
of power was not effectively developed until the second
quarter of the nineteenth century. In the last quarter
came electric power, and finally—only within the present
generation—the widespread use of gasoline. Coal, oil
and hydro-electric power have, of course, increased the
output of all kinds of goods at an unbelievable rate. But
the end is not yet in sight, for science will surely discover

new ways of producing power even more cheaply than today, which, in turn, will still further cheapen mechanical production and transportation and hence increase the output of new goods.

Through the three-fold combination of metals, horse-power and machinery, the cost of production in countless lines has been steadily reduced. The effect of this on the scale of living of millions of people is marked. Lowered costs have made it possible to sell goods at lower prices. Reduced prices have enabled more people to buy more goods and thus to have a larger share in the good things of life. This has increased consumption, necessitating a larger volume of output. This, in turn, has meant more work for more people, and more profits.

Consumption, in the final analysis, rests on the power to buy. The power to buy out of a fixed income is largely determined by the prices at which the needed or desired goods sell. Ninety-nine out of every hundred families in America live on incomes that are more or less fixed—and that average scarcely $1,800 a year. The more they can buy for each of their dollars, the better off they are. The less they can get for each dollar, the more restricted is their existence. In other words, low prices enable them to buy more; higher prices mean that they can buy less.

The relation of low prices to buying power has not, until recently, been sufficiently stressed. Instead, most emphasis has been put on the need of increasing wages. While larger pay, of course, contributes to the wage-earner's feeling of prosperity, and in many lines of work has long been over-due, benefits are restricted to the recipients of the pay increases, whereas lower prices are of benefit to everyone. This point has been effectively brought out by Dr. Harold G. Moulton, in his interesting book, "Income and Economic Progress." He shows that the number of industrial workers, although large, represents only a comparatively small portion of the wage-earners of the country. Those whose wages are raised can, of course, buy more with their increased income—provided prices do not rise. But those whose wages are not raised do not share in the benefits.

Price reduction, in contrast, helps everyone, whether or not his wages are raised. This is why a sound and logical economic policy must necessarily be based on lowering prices. It goes without saying that price reduction should be effected by the use of improved technological and organizational methods and not by reducing wages. The automobile industry—to name but one of many—has shown that it is possible to lower costs of production year by year and at the same time actually to increase wages and employ more people. These lower costs make it possible to sell goods more cheaply—and hence in larger volume—while the producers still make good profits. Henry Ford is the classical exponent of this principle.

In agriculture this theory has long been applied by efficient farmers. The use of improved strains of plants and animals, and better adaptation of crops to soil facilities, has made it possible to obtain larger yields per acre without correspondingly increasing the amount of labor or other items in the cost of production. Thus has the old ideal of making two blades of grass grow where only one grew before been realized—and it has well repaid those who have applied it.

An economy of abundance rests on the sound concept that the benefits of increased cheaper production must be shared. This, in turn, imposes the obligation on the nation's scientific, industrial and political leaders to seek out new ways by which more goods and new kinds of goods can be produced and distributed more cheaply. Such a policy is the exact opposite of the philosophy of restriction and of limiting output and making a thirty-hour week mandatory. It calls for more markets, both at home and abroad, and for the discovery of new ways to satisfy old wants. It assumes confidently that men will continue to devise things which, like the radio or cheap automobiles, will be bought by millions of families, and that thus vast new industries will be established, bringing new work—and new satisfactions—to millions. Only defeatists can accept the philosophy of restriction.

This theory of increased production is often criticized on the ground that production—too much production—was responsible for the great depression of 1929. From this it is argued that production must henceforth be strictly rationed and planned.

This is a misreading of economic history. The great depression was due, not to over-production, but to under-consumption—not to the output of more goods than the world could use, but to the failure of many persons to continue to buy the goods which they were accustomed to use. They wanted them and still needed them, but, for various reasons, their power to buy was curtailed. The closing of long-established European markets resulted in a piling up of unsold goods in America. These temporary surpluses were what depressed the prices of raw materials and so brought the world agricultural crisis to a head—a crisis made all the more cruel by the fact that millions starved for the food which the farmers were unable to sell.

Nations are much like individuals when it comes to buying things and paying for them. Men must work in order to earn enough to buy what they need. When men are thrown out of work, or cannot sell what they have produced, their income is cut and they are forced to reduce their purchases. If they continue unemployed for long, and lack means of self-subsistence, their ability to consume remains small. The cure for this is not to limit production, but to enable more men to produce more things and so to increase their earnings and their spending power. Instead of accepting temporary under-consumption as permanent, the objective should be increased production at lower costs with consequent lower prices for everyone.

The necessary emphasis on cheaper methods of manufacture should not deflect attention from the importance of improving and cheapening the methods of distribution. Many of the services of middlemen, agents and advertisers are indispensable, and to this extent are justifiable additions to the price at which a product or a service sells. But economists are largely in accord in thinking that much can be done to lower prices by economies in methods of distribution. The subject is so controversial and as yet so inadequately explored that few ready generalizations about it can be made other than the assertion that distribution is the weakest link in the economic chain.

It will help toward clearer thinking about national problems to generalize that, just as production is the key to new wealth, so there is a direct relation between production, profits and savings. In fact, it might be said that the logical sequence is: production—profits—savings—capital—new production. In other words, out of what is produced a part is profits; of this a part is saved; this, in turn, if used to facilitate the production of more goods, becomes capital in the form of machinery, factories, tools and other things used in the creation of new wealth which are not themselves consumed or worn out in the process of production.

Put in plain English, a hoe used to cultivate a garden represents capital. It was originally acquired as a result of saving and lasts for many years. This is one of the characteristics of capital—that it represents accumulation or deferred use, and that it has a long period of utility. A head of cabbage, in contrast, grown in the garden cultivated by the hoe, is used up when it is eaten. Economists refer to cabbages as "consumers' goods" and to hoes—or factories, or shoe machines—as "capital goods." One is used up at once, the other endures perhaps for years. One serves an immediate need. The other helps provide for future needs.

The purpose in stressing this is to drive home the lesson that capital is as old as mankind. Incidentally, so also is a return on capital. It is true that, technically speaking, interest—the "hiring" of capital—is comparatively new. But income from the productive use of capital is as old as the plowed field or the domestication of animals. A herd of dairy cattle may be regarded as capital and the milk that they yield may be called income. So also, the field that has been plowed and seeded represents capital. The crop from that field is a direct form of income.

The relation of production to profits is clear. Without production there can be no profits. Without profits there will be little production, for the simple reason that men are reluctant to work unless they obtain from their labor something that they can use to their own advantage. Men go into business to earn a living. The only way they can earn a living out of business is by making more from what they sell—whether it be goods or services—than it costs them to run their business. This is their margin of profit. When they can no longer find buyers for their products or services at a price which still allows them a profit, they are forced to suspend or go out of business. Without profits—except for a comparatively short time—they must close shop.

Failure to understand this aspect of profits is one of the reasons why there has been so much foolish talk about "abolishing the profit motive." As in so many similar proposals the reasoning is as superficial as it is mistaken. Because exorbitant profits are anti-social it is assumed that all profits are anti-social. The truth is, of course, that reasonable profits not only are proper but are absolutely indispensable. The need is to check the abuses of the profit system—not to scrap the system itself.

Equally absurd is the widely popularized doctrine that the modern industrial business system prevents— I use the words of a collectivist writer—"the liberation of the abundance which industry is now capable of producing." What this means, in simple terms, is that business could produce much more than at present but that it does not wish to do so—in other words that business men are deliberately denying the people those goods which the people want and need.

The reasoning by which the believers in this myth reach their conclusion is apparently as follows: Big business, they say, is an evil; business men are selfish; therefore the failure of the people to get what they want is due to the wickedness and selfishness of business. Wealth is concentrated in the hands of a few people. The means of production, *i.e.*, the factories and plants—are owned by a mere fraction of the population. When these owners shut down their plants or refuse to lower prices they do so because they do not want the people to have what they produce.

Some of the premises in this statement are correct, but the conclusions are wrong and misleading. It is true that many business men are selfish and that they want to make as much money as they can. It is true that industrial ownership is concentrated in the hands of a comparatively few people. When the owners shut down their plants there is often a shortage of goods. But owners and producers do not stop production for some purely arbitrary reason like a desire to withhold goods from buyers. The one thing that every sensible industrialist wants is a good, steady—and increasing—market for his products. What he dreads above all else is the failure of consumers to buy. He seeks, therefore, to increase sales —not to reduce them. His interest is in a policy of abundance, not in a policy of scarcity. What this requires is not a low but a high purchasing power by the people—not a shortage of sales but a steady increase of sales. This, in turn, calls for more production.

Production is the lifeblood of business. Only by production can the economic needs of the world be supplied —and the process of production continues from the initial growth or extraction of the raw material until the consumer finally buys and uses the finished article. The only wealth in the world besides raw materials is the stored-up fruit of production. The milled flour on the grocer's shelf represents the work of countless men. So does the suit the worker wears. Had men not raised the wheat and sheep and made the flour and wool, there would be no stock on the grocer's shelf, no suit on the worker's back. Someone—in these days many people using many machines—worked to produce the raw materials and transform them step by step into the final products for daily use.

Because of this part played by men in producing goods it has been argued that labor is chiefly responsible for the finished products and that, therefore, labor is entitled to the major portion—or to all—of the profits from the sale of these products. Like so many other social-economic doctrines, this is the outcome of faulty reasoning. It starts from the premise that many workers are underpaid and that, especially before and in the early days of the industrial revolution, they were, as a group, grossly imposed upon and made to work excessive hours for a mere pittance. The argument is that labor is responsible for all the improvements through which raw materials are put when they are processed or manufactured and that, therefore, labor is being defrauded when a part of the profits are diverted to others.

Let us look at the facts:

1. Labor, especially in the earlier days, was shock-

ingly underpaid. In many industries today wages are still too low. This part of the premise is thus correct.

2. But when the assertion that the increased values which raw materials acquire when they are manufactured are due solely to labor is examined, the fallacy is at once apparent. A century ago, the assertion was largely correct. Labor—hand work—was the basis of all manufacture. But today machines and motive power have taken the place of labor. Their work—not the work of the masses—is largely responsible for the new wealth created out of raw materials.

Take even the simple case of a steam shovel. It is true that the operator must acquire considerable skill to handle it properly. But the value of the work it performs lies largely in its power to move in a few hours a mass of material which not even a hundred men with picks and shovels could move in that time.

Most of the iron ore out of which steel is made is mined by machinery; all of it is transported by machinery; the ore is mechanically smelted; the furnaces are now for the most part machine stoked; from beginning to end machines do the work and men the directing and controlling. What share of the profits rightly belongs to the steel workers? What share to the machines?

The truth is that the old idea that the wealth of the world is the product of the exploitation of the world's workers is no longer correct. Wealth nowadays is the product of the exploitation of the world's natural resources by machines devised by man's ingenuity and operated by horsepower extracted, directly or indirectly, from the earth. Capital is not, as Lincoln believed, the stored-up fruit of labor, though in his day, this definition was largely correct. It is the stored-up product of mines, machines and men—with the principal emphasis on the first two.

It is only natural that, as a result of the gigantic increase of capital in the last century, and the increasing attacks on the evils of the industrial system under the name of capitalism, there should be much confusion between the terms "capital" and "capitalism." Capital, as already explained, is the stored-up fruit of past production, such as factories or railroads, or the known undeveloped supplies of raw materials which can be used at will —like farm lands, forests, mines or oil wells. Capitalism, as the term is commonly used, is a form of economic society in which the means of production are owned by a small proportion of the population and the great mass of mankind is forced to work for these owners. Capitalism is not an outgrowth of capital. Rather is it a result of the developments of the industrial revolution which, at the same time that it increased many-fold the volume of new wealth produced, facilitated the concentration and control of new capital in a few hands.

While this is nothing new—in nearly every known economic system a comparatively few men have managed to obtain control of the means of production and the workers of the world have served them—capitalism has, by the development of machine industry, succeeded in concentrating the means of production geographically as well as economically, and so has led to even greater centralization of wealth and economic power than existed in most previous periods of the world's history. In the last century, in particular, the trend has been toward the substitution of vast corporations for small businesses. The legal structure and position of corporations has facilitated and encouraged this process. At the same time, the mechanization of production has greatly increased the dependence of the masses on factories for work.

To be sure, industrial capitalism, by way of compensation, has brought to the masses enormous material advantages. Articles which were regarded as the luxurious privileges of the very wealthy only two generations ago are now enjoyed by countless millions. But as a result of the factory system, there exists today in Great Britain, and, to a lesser extent in America, a proletariat almost as large and dependent as that in Rome at its worst—a true proletariat, made up of men and women without property, without assured steady work, dependent for their very survival on the acts of impersonal corporate employers.

While this condition did not originate under industrial capitalism, it has become worse under it. Failure of business leaders to do much to remedy it has lent

76

plausibility to the charge that business is indifferent to the workers and thrives by exploiting them. The truth is, of course, that business, considered as a whole, has usually taken every possible advantage of the workers. It has been short-sighted, selfish and inhuman. Even those corporations which have provided for the material comfort of their employees have failed to recognize their spiritual needs. In particular, few, if any, adjustments have been made to the worker's constant fear of losing his job—a fear so strong as to be stultifying and morally corrosive. Many businesses have, in fact, grown fat by exploiting this fear. Rare indeed have been those employers who have removed this fear by insuring efficient, loyal workers life tenure of their jobs.

Men like to "belong"—they like to feel that they are needed, and that their work is appreciated. When, as is so often the case in large corporations, the average employee is little more than a number—at best a commodity —his sense of service is atrophied. Most men throughout the ages have, of course, worked for wages or their equivalent in kind. They have thus been dependent on others for their livelihood. But before the development of great factories and corporations there was usually a personal element in the relationship of worker and employer, and a personal attitude toward the work on the part of both. The employer felt a distinct sense of responsibility for his employee's welfare. The workman had keen interest, if not actual pride, in his work.

Today, the economic concept of labor as a commodity has been degraded into the inhuman concept of the laborer as a mere tool. To the extent that a "hand" has to sell his services, the economic concept is technically defensible. But the failure to think of the laborer as a human being, and to treat him as such, has made the modern industrial system the harshest and most inhuman relationship yet devised by man in the Western world. The average workman feels that he is no more than a wheel or a bolt in a machine—and as easily replaced. To him, his work is something to be got through with—not to perform with pride. The boss, instead of being a human being, is separated from the worker by the barriers of business caste. The boss's interest is in profits, not in the human equation. To him, the average worker is on a par with the average machine—some are more efficient than others, but all are equally inhuman.

What the cure for this evil may be is far from clear. In theory, some form of joint responsibility would seem desirable—involving not only a sharing of profits but also of losses. The workers suffer as much from inefficient management as the owners—if not more. The owners, if the business is badly conducted and fails, lose their savings. The workers lose their jobs—and this loss of a job is, to the average worker, a calamity far greater than the loss of savings to the average business man. Workers and owners are thus alike interested in seeing that a business be so run that an even balance of earnings can be maintained in lean as in fat years. To do this requires great managerial skill as well as a large measure of co-operation between owners and employees.

Much has been written about the evils of the divorce between ownership and operation—absentee ownership of industry to parallel absentee landlordism. In so far as it has resulted in making owners feel little or no responsibility for the conduct of their business, it is bad. But the fact must be faced that most stockholders are not in a position to know anything about the business in which they hold shares and, even if told, would be incompetent to pass wise judgment on policies. This is why management has come to be regarded as trusteeship. In fairness to management, it should be said that it has usually acquitted itself honorably.

Of greater menace than mere absentee ownership is absentee control for ulterior purposes—*i.e.*, acquisition of one business by another in order to destroy it or to establish a monopoly or to build up a great combination. In particular the operations of private bankers and lawyers in reorganizations have often produced serious evils. The trouble arises from the inevitable ignorance of bankers and lawyers about technical business problems—an ignorance which is not compensated by the hiring of experts, for the reason that too often the experts are consulted but not heeded. Furthermore, when a man has an active participation in the direction of a dozen big corporations, he cannot possibly give proper attention to any one. The result is that management, as a rule, is unrestrained, and the interests of the directors are likely only to be aroused when combinations are to be effected. Often these are proper and sound, but often also they are designed to further the interests of groups other than the owners of the company, or the workers in it. Even when the purposes are proper and the economic results justifiable, the concentrations of economic power thus effected can be highly dangerous to the social and political, as well as to the economic and financial, body. However forceful the economic arguments in favor of gigantic business combinations, the social arguments are overwhelmingly against them and in favor of decentralization.

That capitalism, like other systems, contains the seeds of its own destruction is obvious. Unless the trend toward concentration of ownership and control can be reversed, and unless relations with employees can be placed on a human basis, the system is almost sure to be superseded by another. It remains to be seen, therefore, if the leaders of modern business, industry and finance possess the vision and intelligence to meet the new needs constructively, and if they are able to extort sufficient cooperation from government to prevent the system from sinking under the weight of bureaucratic parasitism.

The tendency of bureaucrats to fatten on big business is nothing new. Always the rich, when they have not controlled government, have been the prey of politicians.

Plato has described the traditional attempts to squeeze as much honey from them as possible. In the days of Rome, the great fortunes were levied upon, directly or indirectly, by the Emperors. Big business of today is like the rich in the old days. It is being devoured by the politicians. The question is not whether business should or should not be taxed, but whether such heavy—or such foolish—taxes will be imposed as to force many businesses to the wall.

On the part of government, the responsibility is to be reasonable and just; on the part of business to be fair, honest and far-sighted. In recent years, government has inclined to unreasonable meddling, and business men have condoned practices which they knew were wrong. In the resultant struggles between politicians and business leaders, the rights of the consuming public have been ignored. If only government and business alike could learn the lesson that the interests of politicians, business men, bankers and consumers would all be benefited by uniting in a policy of working toward lower prices and increased production, America would resume the realization of its early ideal of bringing as large a share of the good things of the world to as many families as possible. Cheaper goods mean a demand for more goods. More goods mean more work and more profits. This is the path to prosperity. Restriction is the road to ruin.

THE AMERICAN WAY

VI

WHAT THE FATHERS FOUNDED

The framers of the American Constitution were essentially practical men. Their task was to devise a federal government that would work in the United States of 1787. They dared not depart too far from colonial precedents and experience, as they feared that political innovations might turn the people against the new plan. The conflicting interests of different groups and sections had to be adjusted and opposing ideas about forms of government had to be harmonized. Hence compromises were frequent in their deliberations and determined the precise form of their final proposal. From the beginning to the end, they had to check the desirable by the possible, the ideal by the practicable.

That the Constitution which they drew up left much to be desired was as clear to them as it has been to subsequent students of government. It is doubtful if any single delegate approved of all the provisions of the document. Many signers disliked particular sections. But they expected that the plan would be modified—as in fact it has been. Through all the debates the idea that new conditions would require new departures was clearly accepted. They had no thought that the Constitution was final and definitive, and that it was so far superior to other schemes of government that it would endure unchanged forever. All that they dared hope was that by outlining certain general principles of government, leaving the details to subsequent determination, they could establish the framework of a government which would make possible that "more perfect union" without which, in their belief, the American states could not survive. Many of the framers were doubtful about the proposed government. Some were pessimistic. But they were agreed in believing that the new plan was better than the loose confederation that existed after the Revolution, and they were eager to give it a trial on the chance that it would save the Union—and the states—and insure order and stability for a number of years.

At this distant date, it is hard to realize how compelling was the need for a "more perfect union" in 1787. It was, in fact, the dominant force behind those who framed the Constitution and who urged its adoption. Beneath the weight of this argument, their own objections and the objections of doubters and opponents of many details of the document were crushed. The signers were convinced that, without a more perfect union between the states, their hard-won independence would be lost. They knew that the confederation as it then existed did not function and could not endure. They feared that even if the states escaped re-annexation to England, they would, unless firmly united, follow the discordant example of Europe and create a group of warring little nations. Bound together by an effective government they hoped to become a great nation. Disjointed they faced disaster.

In re-reading contemporary records, it is striking how completely men who, like Alexander Hamilton of New York, and Edmund Randolph of Virginia, disapproved important provisions of the Constitution, subordinated their own views and made inspiring defenses of the document because of their conviction that its ratification was essential to the very existence of the thirteen states. Hamilton is known to have had such scant sympathy for the work of the Philadelphia convention, to which he was a delegate, that he took little part in its deliberations. Yet his arguments in its defense, both in the pages of the "Federalist" and at the state convention at Poughkeepsie when New York considered ratification, are among the most brilliant and convincing expositions of the advantages of the Constitution ever made. Randolph, who refused to sign at Philadelphia the Constitution which he had been active in framing, later fought valiantly for it at the Virginia convention. It is strange that these two men who were distrustful of many parts of the plan should have been largely responsible for its acceptance by two states which seemed bound to reject it. Had Hamilton and Randolph allowed their prejudices to override their conviction that the Constitution, despite its faults, must be adopted if the Union were to be saved, the course of world history would have been changed. There is little doubt that if New York and Virginia had failed to ratify the Constitution, it would never have been put into effect.

That the delegates assembled in Philadelphia represented the wishes of the people at large is unlikely for the simple reason that, despite active participation in the war for independence, most Americans were at that time but little interested in politics or in questions of government. Even the catchwords "liberty" and "independence" had lost much of their magic as the chaos following the war made it doubtful that the advantages of separation from Britain were as great as the leaders of the Revolution had proclaimed. Many of the people were, of course, illiterate. The majority had had little or no schooling. When, therefore, political problems were forced on their attention they were content to follow their local leaders—often men whom they knew personally. These local leaders, in turn, accepted the views of those who, through heritage, wealth or ambition, held or coveted offices in the state governments. National leadership thus naturally fell into the hands of men of education and property. Equally naturally, therefore, men of education and property framed the Constitution.

In a civilization in which social inequalities were inconspicuous there was little or no class consciousness on the part of the founding fathers. Glaring disparities of income were rare in the United States of 1787. Nearly any one who had energy could acquire property. The leaders in the law, the ministry and business—in other words, the influential citizens in each community—were, many of them, of plain origin. Standards of living, except in Philadelphia, New York, Baltimore, Charleston, and the southern plantations, were frugal. Social tolerance was wide because men made a competence easily, and merit and ability were readily recognized and rewarded. The delegates looked upon themselves as trustees for the people of their states—not as spokesmen for particular groups. They had constantly in mind the general welfare of the people as a whole, regardless of social standing or of economic status.

To the extent that the framers believed that "the well born"—by which they meant men of education and position—had the duty to take part in politics, their point of view may be described as "aristocratic." But they were themselves too close to simple origins to think in terms of anything but a "natural aristocracy" based on the concept that differences in ability and circumstances give to some men the responsibility, if not the right, to rule. To the extent that they distrusted the capacity of illiterate or almost completely uneducated men to judge intelligently about intricate political questions, and so believed that the privilege of voting should be restricted, the framers were "anti-democratic." But the rights secured under the Constitution were for all men, regardless of whether or not they could vote, and the government which the founders proposed was more genuinely popular than any system then existing in the world.

Even though the form of government established by the delegates to the Federal Convention was, according to political standards of the day, "advanced," if not actually "radical," it was not a democracy in the true sense of the word—not a government in which all the people assemble to take direct action in specific cases. In fact, although clearly a government *for* the people, it was rather a government *with the consent of* the governed than *by* the governed. What the framers proposed was a representative republic, in which the people delegate to agents of their own choice the authority to exercise for a limited period specific powers deliberately checked and restricted by a written constitution. It was of the very essence of this system that the people should choose their own agents and should be able to turn them out of office at stated periods if they failed to carry out the popular will. It was also of its very essence that the authority entrusted to these agents should be checked and balanced so that no individual or group could ever become all-powerful. But the founders did not anticipate universal suffrage, and tried to guard against direct elections save for the House of Representatives. They confidently expected that theirs would be, in fact, a government of the best, and that to the high offices in the Federal government would be attracted men of intelligence, character and property.

Lest modern readers feel that the framers' fears of the abuses of power by those in office were exaggerated, it should be borne in mind that to the men of 1787, arbitrary personal government was something very real and very much to be dreaded and avoided. They knew from their own experience under the British crown how prone men in power are to misuse their offices and how easily rulers whose authority is unrestrained become arbitrary and seek to rob the people of their freedom, their property and their rights. To the framers of the Constitution, freedom was precious, having been dearly bought in the war; property was the foundation on which their hopes for the betterment of themselves and their children was based, and so was to be made safe beyond any possible doubt; and their rights were so valuable that they must be preserved at all costs—even by fighting, if need be. In their minds, the greatest danger to their freedom lay in the weakness of the confederacy. The menace to their property resided in political disorder and economic instability. The threat to their rights lay in the possibility of falling under arbitrary rulers. Hence they wanted a government that would be effective but restrained, that would guarantee public order and secure property, and that would make it impossible for men in office to exercise arbitrary power and so to endanger those basic civil liberties which to the framers seemed sacred and unalienable.

It was only natural that the members of the Federal

Convention turned to their own experience in the state and colonial governments and adapted and combined forms of government which to the people were already familiar. In addition they drew on history for suggestions or for confirmation. In so far as mere theory affected their deliberations the writing of Montesquieu, and to a lesser extent of Blackstone, had the greatest influence. Among the delegates, James Madison alone had the professorial mind, but it was his genius to base his speculative thought on a voluminous reading of history and to check every proposal by reference to past experience. James Wilson and Alexander Hamilton were conspicuous for their grasp of governmental principles. Most of the other delegates brought a varied knowledge drawn from the school of experience, with an ample background of English history and colonial politics as well as a thorough knowledge of particular problems in their own states. Daily their deliberations were presided over by the silent but awe-inspiring General Washington—a man whose common sense was as supreme as his character. Washington took no part in the formal debates. But under his stern eye men acted with earnestness and restraint. He inspired moderation and reason and by his example discouraged pettiness and selfishness. Men knew he had the nation's interests at heart. He was above countenancing any sly schemes to entrench a single group in power, or to help avaricious men make fortunes illicitly. His presence at the convention was as much of a safeguard to the deliberations as his approval of the final document was a guarantee of its soundness.

Fundamental in the political practice as well as the theory of the America of that day was the doctrine of the separation of powers. Contrary to some of the modern interpretations of the Constitution, this separation was not intended to be rigid. By connecting and blending the functions of the executive, legislative and judicial branches of the new government, it was expected that each would serve as a check against attempted abuses by the others. No branch was to possess, directly or indirectly, an overruling influence over the others in the administration of their respective powers. When Hamilton explained the system to the New York ratifying convention, he remarked that "the legislative authority is lodged in three distinct branches; the executive authority is divided between two branches; and the judicial is still reserved for an independent body, who hold their office during good behavior." The making of laws required the concurrence of the two houses of Congress and of the President. The making of treaties and appointments to high office required the concurrence of the Senate and the President. The judiciary alone was independent, except in so far as the judges were chosen by the President with the advice and consent of the Senate, and that they might be impeached by the Congress.

This blending of powers served the double purpose of increasing efficiency and yet of holding the branches in check. Contrary to the claims of certain modern historians, the eagerness of the framers to insure the establishment of effective checks was not alone due to the theoretic teachings of Montesquieu. It grew out of their passionate desire to make it impossible for any man or group of men in office to take to themselves arbitrary powers. They believed that a legislative body unrestrained was just as likely to be tyrannical as a king or dictator. As the "Federalist" put it, "the accumulation of all powers, legislative, executive, and judiciary, in the same hands, whether of one, a few, or many, and whether hereditary, self-appointed, or elective, may justly be pronounced the very definition of tyranny."

The method which the framers used to prevent the accumulation of these powers in one branch of the government was ingenious. As they knew from experience the readiness of legislative bodies to pass unwise or unjust laws, they divided the Federal legislature into two branches, one of which, the Senate, was expected to serve as a brake on the impetuosity of the other. Where the members of the House were to be directly chosen by popular vote and to hold office only two years, the Senators were to be chosen by their state legislatures and to hold office for six years. A constant change of Congressmen was expected, but it was hoped that the Senators would be reelected and so become, in effect, a group of elder statesmen. While having important legislative functions, they were expected to be close to the President through sharing with him the treaty-making and appointive powers.

The President, while given the power of vetoing laws, was nevertheless subjected to the important qualification that his veto could be overridden. Empowered to nominate appointive officers of the government, his selections were nevertheless subject to confirmation by the Senate. Thus he was partly to be held in check by Congress, and partly, in turn, to hold that body in check. That he would ever become all-powerful did not apparently occur to the founders. They feared the excessive concentration of powers in Congress rather than in the executive. They dreaded parliamentary government rather than Presidential government.

The judiciary branch was, by its very nature, the most independent of the three. Much of its work was expected to be technical. But the right of the Supreme Court to deny the constitutionality of an act of Congress or of a state legislature was not only implied in the Constitution as actually worded, but was fully explained in the "Federalist" and in arguments in behalf of the ratification of the Constitution. From the beginning, therefore, the courts were expected to interpret the Constitution. The reasoning was simple—that the Constitution is the supreme law of the land, superior to all statutory laws, whether passed by Congress or the states; that, as the Constitution provides that the Supreme Court shall have jurisdiction over all cases arising under the Constitution as well as under the laws of the United States, it becomes the Supreme Court's natural duty, when there is an apparent conflict between a law and the Constitution, to declare whether the statute in question is or is not constitutional. But this power, it should be noted, is neither general nor all-embracing. The Supreme Court has never taken cognizance of the constitutionality of a law except when a particular lawsuit challenging a particular act has been brought before it. The judges do not decide questions. They only decide cases. They do not pass on the wisdom or desirability of legislation. They consider only whether or not a particular part of a particular act which has been challenged in the courts is constitutional. Even this they can only do when a case is brought before them in which one of the litigants rests his position on a right based on a provision of the Constitution and the other contends the contrary.

The framers never intended that the Supreme Court should sit on the sidelines of Congress and say, "This law is constitutional, this one is not." The courts have never exercised any power to make laws or change them or alter the form of government. They cannot even suggest or formulate policies. They cannot be called upon in advance to express opinions as to the validity of an act of Congress. Their advice on legislation may not be sought. Any observations which they may make about laws are purely incidental to the determination of the case before the court.

That the Constitution was a mixture of various principles and philosophies of government was inevitable. But it is a mark of the wisdom and vision of the founders that, even though they based their plan on a frank distrust of the ability of the mass of the people—particularly of those who were without education and could not even read or write—to govern themselves, the whole system rested on the consent of the governed and was designed not only to give the people effective control over their rulers but also to protect the people from arbitrary acts by their rulers. The framers founded their system on the theory that government derives all its powers directly or indirectly from the great body of the people, not from any particular class. They expected the Federal machine to be administered by men holding office for a limited period, and subject to removal for bad behavior. Repeatedly in the ratification debates, it was pointed out that, as the source of all power resides in the people as a whole, it is the people's right to alter or abolish the Constitution as they see fit.

The framers made a sharp distinction between, on the one hand, a constitution, which is established by the people and which cannot be altered by the government, and, on the other hand, a mere law, which is established by the government and which the government itself can alter. One of the chief reasons why ratification and amendment of the Constitution was left to the people and not to Congress was the determination of the framers

to preserve particular rights to the people and to hold
the governors in check. Had the framers made it possible for the Congress and the President to alter the Constitution without the assent of the people, it is obvious
that the government could in short order have scrapped
the Constitution as it was originally drawn up and have
taken to itself all those powers which were expressly denied to it by the Constitution.

It was expected, *per contra*, that laws would be easily
changed or repealed. One act of Congress has often an-
nulled or changed another. But the founders knew that
legislatures, moved by mob hysteria, could be driven
to enact laws which were unjust, undesirable and unenforceable. They therefore determined that the Constitution itself should not be thus easily altered—and the
reason was not so much to rivet a particular form of
government on the nation as to protect the people from
their political agents.

Whichever way we turn, we see the eagerness of the
framers to establish a constitution that would govern
the governors as well as the people, and that, by setting
fixed limits on the authority of the governors, would prevent them from becoming all-powerful. This distrust of
men in office was deeply ingrained in the founding
fathers. They knew how power feeds on power, and how
ready any man or group in office is to reach out for more
power. They also knew that unless government could be
held in check, its natural tendency to revert to mastery

would make it difficult, if not impossible, to perpetuate the civil liberties which the framers valued above all else. Power unrestrained—not power carefully limited and restricted—was what they feared. Hence their attempts to make a constitution which would be superior to the whims of men, and to establish rules of government which would apply to rich and poor, rulers and ruled, alike.

Their work is all the more remarkable when it is realized that, as James Wilson pointed out to the Pennsylvania ratifying convention, this gathering in Philadelphia in 1787 was "the first instance, as far as we can learn, of a nation unattacked by external force, unconvulsed by domestic insurrections, assembling voluntarily, deliberating fully, and deciding calmly, concerning that system of government under which they would wish that they and their posterity should live."

VII

THE ESSENCE OF FEDERALISM

THE GOVERNMENT which the framers of the Constitution established was federal. It was not a centralized government.

The distinction is fundamental. A federal system is one in which limited powers have been surrendered by the constituent states to a national government. In the American system those powers not specifically granted to the Federal government or prohibited to the states are retained by the states. In contrast, a centralized system is one in which a supreme central government has all powers, and delegates to its political subdivisions only such authority as it is willing to grant them. Decentralization and cooperation are of the essence of federalism. Concentration and subordination characterize a central government.

In a federal system neither the national government nor the states may trespass in the other's allotted sphere of authority. The framers of the American Constitution deliberately curtailed the powers of the Federal government so as to prevent it from interfering too much with the states. In a centralized system, the authority granted to the states or provinces by the omnipotent central government may at will be revoked or curtailed. A federal system, *per contra,* is based on the separate existence of the states. It is, in the famous phrase of Justice Salmon P. Chase, an "indestructible union composed of indestructible states." The union cannot be destroyed except, of course, by civil war. So also the states cannot be destroyed. Their political duties and responsibilities cannot be taken from them by the Federal government. In a centralized national system the local units are subordinate to the central government, and dependent on it. The tendency of a centralized government is to wipe out local differences. The purpose of federalism is to preserve a large measure of local autonomy and to perpetuate local characteristics and protect local interests from national domination.

The history and traditions of the thirteen original states precluded the establishment of a centralized national government in 1787. The exact division of the powers that were to be given to the new government by the states presented one of the most difficult problems which the Constitutional Convention had to solve. Nearly all the delegates opposed substituting a unified central government for the states. When finally the Constitution was offered for ratification, the strongest opposition came, not from any economic class or social group, but from those who wished the states to retain all their powers. The inhabitants of the thirteen states thought of themselves primarily as New Yorkers, or Virginians, or Pennsylvanians, and only incidentally as Americans. While some of them had fought in the Revolution in the name of American independence and had reluctantly joined in a loose confederacy, their loyalty was to their states rather than to the nation. The citizens of each state were jealous of the other states. The small states feared the big ones. The large states were contemptuous of the little ones. At the Federal Convention it required much patience and ingenuity to reconcile these two groups. The solution, as every schoolboy has been taught, was to give the states equal representation in the Senate, and to apportion the members of the House according to population. Thus in the Senate the small states had as much influence as the large, whereas in the House the large states had the advantage of larger delegations.

In one important respect the new government departed from previous Federal forms. Under the Articles of Confederation, as well as in the few historic examples of federalism, the central authority could only deal with the governments of the constituent units. It could not exercise any direct authority over the citizens of the states. The representatives of the thirteen states in the Continental Congress, for example, were little more than ambassadors of their respective states. They not only had no direct authority over the people of the nation as a whole but could not even bind their own governments. In fact, they were so powerless that the decisions of the Continental Congress not only carried no weight with the people but were usually ignored if not actually spurned by the state governments whose representatives had made them.

Under the new American plan the Federal government was to have direct relations with individuals. Men thus were to become citizens of the United States as well as being citizens of a particular state. They were to be subject to Federal laws as well as to the laws of the states. The Federal government even was given the power to tax the citizens of all the states and so to raise revenues independently of the pleasure of the state governments—a relationship calculated to make the Federal government less dependent on the states than in the old confederation.

This establishment of two separate but coordinate governments—Federal and state—exercising authority almost independently over the same citizens, provided a radical departure in political procedure. The idea was not hard to popularize, however, as even before the Revolution the colonists had begun to think of their own colonial governments as something apart from the British crown government at the same time that they recognized the jurisdiction of the crown in many matters. But the deliberate acceptance of two concurrent governments and the formal establishment of dual citizenship which is basic in the American system was something new in its day, and still seems incomprehensible to many European students of government.

103

It was characteristic of the framers' project that while the Federal government was to have no direct authority over the state governments, the state governments were given important functions in the maintenance of the Federal government. True, the Constitution itself controlled the state constitutions and state laws, and no state law could run counter to a Federal law. But all suggestions that the Federal government be authorized to negative state laws by some sort of veto were rejected. The state legislatures were given a direct part in the selection of one important branch of the Federal government—the Senate—and, under the original terms of the Constitution had a controlling voice in the choice of the President. In fact, so dependent was the new government on the states that it may properly be called the creature of the states, even though its powers derive, in the final analysis, from the consent of the people. The state governments, by contrast, were in large measure independent of the Federal government.

The need for defining the respective powers of the two governments in a federal system is one of the principal reasons why a written constitution is indispensable in such a system. Unless the limits of power are clearly outlined, there are sure to be unending quarrels about authority.

The general principle which the framers followed in trying to draw the difficult boundary between the two spheres of authority was to assign to the Federal government only such powers as were necessary for dealing with problems that transcended state lines, leaving to the states full powers to deal with all local problems. While the delegates do not appear to have formulated a definite principle in so many words it may be said that their concept was that no larger units of government should perform any functions which could as well or better be performed by smaller units.

The tradition of local self-government was strong in the states. It was not only a heritage from England but embodied the logical experience of a pioneer people. As men made new clearings in the forests and opened up new communities on the frontier, they had to rely on themselves for such simple functions of government as they required. As their communities grew, they joined with other communities for common purposes, and when it was necessary to deal with the colonial or state governments, they sent representatives, not as humble petitioners seeking the grant of favors, but as free men demanding their rights and willing to take their share of the common burdens. They had a keen dislike of the idea of subordination—whether to a distant king in England, or a remote government in Philadelphia, or Washington, but they were ready, albeit sometimes reluctantly, to join with their equals when to do so would serve their own interests. Pioneering fosters independence and self-reliance. A pioneer people is likely to believe firmly that it can run its own affairs better than can distant officials.

The history of the winning of the West suggests that this view was the right view.

To the framers of the Constitution, union did not mean amalgamation. It did not imply the subordination of the states to the Federal government. The term "United States" meant just what it said: states united in a common cause, not states surrendering their independent existence to an all-powerful new central government. In the words of Woodrow Wilson, the states were "self-originated, self-constituted, self-confident, self-sustaining." So much power did they reserve to themselves that it was commonly believed that the states not only could cripple, but could actually destroy, the Federal government. Nationalists like Alexander Hamilton were convinced that there was more danger to the Federal government from the states than to the states from the Federal government. They looked on the latter as weak, the former as strong.

States' rights have been a subject of incessant debate ever since the first union was suggested in 1776. They have caused one major war. The controversy still rages, for there are now, as always, two conflicting concepts of government in the United States—the one that the Federal authority should be extended until it is supreme, and the other that the states should be preserved and even strengthened. The arguments are so well worn that they hardly need repetition. Since the Civil War the tendency toward concentration of more power in the

Federal government has grown steadily. Each decade has seen this concentration intensified—the product of the Federal government's own desire to make itself stronger, and of the loss of interest in state affairs due in part to frequent migrations from state to state and in part to the increasing emphasis in the headlines on national affairs. Most men care little who is governor of the state in which they happen to reside. They care much, however, about who is President. The state governor is often, in the popular mind, a mere pompous politician. The President, in contrast, is a glamorous figure, sitting in the seats of the mighty, the spokesman of the nation, the representative of all the people.

The argument of those who favor still more centralization and who contend that the states are mere relics of the horse-and-buggy days, is that the development of big industries doing business across state lines, and the rapid improvement of communications which has knit the nation closely together, have completely integrated the economic and social life of the country. We are no longer a union of forty-eight states, they say, but a single nation, in which the states not only have ceased to serve a necessary purpose but are actually incapable of performing government functions which are indispensable today. Only the Federal government, it is contended, can deal with the new economic problems because only the Federal government can extend its powers across state lines. Better, in fact, to abolish these state lines and to make the national government supreme, having full authority to exercise all the powers which have heretofore been reserved to the states.

The need of extending the Federal powers was foreshadowed by the founding fathers in their emphasis on the necessity of giving to the Federal government the control of everything pertaining to interstate commerce. This in itself was a realization of the fact that the states could not be entrusted with sole supervision over business. But it goes without saying that they never dreamed of the extent to which commerce—by which they meant what we now call business—would be ramified and interlocked throughout the states. Nor could they possibly foresee how modern methods of transportation and communications would present new problems which the states could not control unaided.

In considering the desirability of empowering the Federal government to do what the states cannot or will not do, two fundamental principles should be borne in mind. The first is that local self-government not only is the basis of the American system, but is indispensable in any truly free government. The second is that the greater the population, the greater the need for decentralization of administration.

The importance of local self-government—by which is meant not only a large measure of autonomy for cities and towns, but also for the states—is two-fold. In the first place, the people of a given region have a greater familiarity with the problems of that region than have outsiders. In the second place, only through local self-government can the people maintain close contact with the politicians. Under local self-government the officials are chosen from the locality. When, in contrast, a great centralized bureaucracy extends its sway over all the country, as, for example, in France, its agents chosen to administer local units are picked with little or no regard for local wishes. It follows that they are usually unknown to the locality and have no real connection with it. Government thus tends to remove itself from the people. In the resulting divorce government is deprived of popular interest and ceases to be, in fact, popular. The fundamental principle that government shall be with the consent of the governed is violated.

The relation of population growth to decentralization has been little understood. This is due to a mistaken conclusion drawn from the geographical unification of the country resulting from improved communications. The common assumption is that, just as before communications were modernized, decentralization was indispensable owing to the difficulty of a central government communicating with distant local regions, so now that time and distance have been annihilated, the need for decentralization has disappeared.

The truth is just the opposite. When a few million people were sparsely scattered along the Atlantic coast the need for binding the country together was paramount. Now that the population has passed 130 millions, the need for decentralizing the country is equally urgent. There are at least two reasons for this: (1) that as population has increased, the demands on government to perform countless services have grown far beyond the poor power of any central bureaucracy to perform them effectively; and (2) that the more complex the local units have become, the more difficult it is for a distant national government to comprehend local problems and to judge wisely about them.

The result of the demands for more services from government has been to increase the clumsiness and the red tape of government administration. Hence as government has grown more unwieldy, it has become more inefficient. The passion of bureaucrats for forms, orders and instructions designed to standardize practices throughout the country and to guide the actions of more or less incompetent subordinates, has made it almost axiomatic that the larger the population over which a government has sway, and the more services which a government seeks to perform, the greater the delays and blunders of administration. Whoever has had contact with government agencies in recent years can bear witness to this truth.

But this is not all. The greater the responsibilities which a government undertakes, the greater is the need for some sort of effective control over government agents if popular government is to be maintained. Without

110

such control, any government, as history clearly shows, tends to abuse its powers. Decentralization offers the desired control, not only because it forces the spread of responsibilities among officials who are directly accountable to the people of a state or local unit, but because it limits the scope of the damage which can result from mistaken action by those high in office.

It should be obvious that a wrong policy imposed on a nation-wide scale can do more damage than one imposed only on a state-wide scale. Independent local units of administration have at least the chance to make and correct their own mistakes. Subordinate units have no alternative but to enforce the mistakes of their superiors. A people governed locally by agents of a distant central government has little influence on the government of its region. But a people which chooses its own agents not only can make its own wishes known through them but can, if the agents persist in acts which the voters do not approve, force the representatives out of office and bring about a change of policies. Locally elected officials dependent on local votes are sure to be much more responsive to local wishes than agents of a central bureaucracy dependent only on some distant bureau chief. In fact, it follows that, just as the local representative will heed local wishes, so the agent of a central government will heed the wishes of that government. His bread and butter depends on the central authority, not the local electorate.

111

The difficulty of a central government in understanding local problems and local needs is so obvious as hardly to need elaboration. Often, even if by chance the local problem is correctly apprehended, the central government's action is determined not by true local needs but by the exigencies of political pressure on bureaucratic administrators. When, on the other hand, a central government makes general rules and tries to apply them rigidly, it produces such absurdities as standardizing the cost of pressing a pair of pants in Jersey City, Reno and Little Rock—without any regard to local conditions.

It would be a perversion of history to pretend that the framers of the Constitution foresaw the many advantages which would inhere in the state system which they perpetuated. But it is a perversion of common sense to assert that the carefully worked out coordination between the states and the Federal government provided in the Constitution is outmoded simply because it was made 150 years ago. Truths are none the less valid because they are old. Political principles and forms which have worked well for long periods have, by the very fact of the success of their past service, a claim for full reexamination before they are discarded or drastically modified merely because of their age.

The remarkable truth is that the founding fathers apparently built far more wisely than they realized when they gave to the world this innovation of a dual government called federalism. As President Franklin D. Roosevelt said of the Constitution in 1932, it is "the most marvellously elastic compilation of the rules of government ever written."

The very fact that the Constitution is a set of rules of government makes it essential that there be an umpire to pass final judgment as to whether or not a particular act of Congress or a state legislature or the act of some official, is constitutional. That such an authority must exist was as clear to the delegates in Philadelphia as it has been to subsequent students of federalism. Without some such arbiter, the Philadelphia plan could not function.

This umpire, as already explained in the last chapter, is the judiciary. In fact, an independent judiciary is one of the pillars of federalism. The power of judicial review may be exercised by any court, state or Federal. It was exercised by a number of the state courts before even the Federal Constitution was framed. It has been exercised frequently by the state courts during the last century and a half. On hundreds of occasions, state courts have had to consider the constitutionality of state laws. But the power of judicial review, it cannot be sufficiently emphasized, is only incidental to the duty of expounding the law when a law is called in question. Only a very few acts of Congress have ever been declared unconstitutional.

Equally fundamental, from a judicial as well as a

113

political point of view, is the right of appeal. This means not only appeal from a lower court to a higher, but also appeal to the courts from the acts of governmental agents. A little thought shows that this right of appeal is of the essence of a free government in which justice is supposed to prevail. When there is no appeal—either from the decision of a lower court or from the acts of an agent of the government—there is no guaranty against arbitrary and unjust oppression. The right was well recognized in Imperial Rome—the Apostle Paul's famous words, "Then I appeal to Cæsar," still thrill the imaginative reader of the book of the Acts.

In England the right of appeal was likewise well established. In revolutionary America it was taken for granted. It is implicit in the Constitution. But in recent years, it has begun to lose its force through the creation of more and more government agencies whose acts are, for all practical purposes, beyond appeal or redress. Even though the legal right of appeal may exist, the cost and complication of making an appeal, except for those with political pull, has, in effect, rendered appeal useless. Too often when appeals are made by uninfluential citizens, they are not even heard or acknowledged—as witness the experience of many citizens in protesting against rulings of the income tax bureaus. A theoretical right of appeal exists. But what can a poor citizen do whose requests for information are not even heeded, and whose appeal can only be made to the same agents who made the questioned ruling? This is obviously no real right of appeal. It is little more than the right to register a futile protest.

The theory underlying the right of appeal is that the citizen should have every opportunity to be protected against injustice on the part of his rulers as well as his fellows. It makes no difference whether an arbitrary or oppressive act be performed by an agent of a majority or by an individual acting on "his own." It is the harmful nature of the act that counts, not the source of power which the agent represents. As Hamilton pointed out on numerous occasions, oppressive acts by majorities are none the less oppressive because a majority sanctions them.

The force of this contention is often overlooked in modern times because so many Americans have accepted without discrimination the common assumption that majorities are always right. This mistaken premise is then twisted into the argument that majorities can do no wrong. From this it is but a step to the proposition that minorities not only must be wrong but have no rights.

This theory is at variance with modern experience and with the philosophy of the Constitution. Mere superiority of numbers does not determine right or wrong. Mathematics applied to politics does not affect the soundness of a policy. All that it records is the preponderant popularity of men and measures of the moment. These men may be wise and their measures good, but the wisdom and soundness are theirs regardless of the size of the popular majority. Often the men are incompetent and the measures bad. History contains many references to wrong policies imposed by majorities as well as by minorities. The confusion of thought apparently arises from mistaking the right of the majority to hold office—which, in the United States, is fundamental—with the false assumption that the majority, because it holds office, is therefore right. A majority can be as wrong as the most pig-headed, selfish minority.

The framers of the Constitution took particular pains to see not only that minorities would be protected from arbitrary acts of majorities, but that the agents of government would be bound to protect minorities at the same time that they carried out the wishes of the majorities. Government in America is for all the people, and not merely for the benefit of the party in power. In fact, inseparable from the concept of representative government is the idea that the elected and appointed agents of the people act as trustees. Their tenure of office is transient, whereas government is enduring. They have power for the period of their election or appointment, but the functions which they perform are continuous and do not cease with a change of officeholders. The temporary control of the machinery of government which has been granted them by the votes of the majority imposes on them the responsibility of acting in the interests of all citizens alike.

The growing disregard of the rights of minorities has strengthened the tendency to belittle the importance of the states' running their own affairs. States have, of course, just as great rights as other minorities to be protected from the interference and dictation of majorities. In fact, local self-government is in itself an expression of a minority right and is persistently implied in the Constitution. The majority of the country may, for the moment, wish to standardize state or municipal administration. But a minority, representing the preponderant body of voters in a particular state or town, may wish to retain its own codes and run its own affairs in its own way. This, so long as the Constitution is in force, it is privileged to do. But if majority rule is to be interpreted to mean that a majority may completely disregard the wishes of minorities this privilege becomes worthless and the devices to protect minorities against majorities cease to function.

The kind of government which the founders devised represents all the people. The people's agents are to act in the best interests of their constituents rather than to do the bidding of a little group of party dictators who regard government as their personal property and who do not recognize that a public office is, in fact as well as in theory, a public trust.

These distinctions, while to a certain extent technical, nevertheless embody a fundamental concept. This is that, just as government derives its powers from the consent of the governed, so the governed retain a large measure of self-determination. The powers that the people have granted in their Constitution they can modify or withdraw. The government that they have created they can overthrow.

The particular value of federalism is that it is expressly designed to give the fullest possible play to self-determination. It accepts as fundamental the right of communities to administer their own affairs. It recognizes that local differences of custom and needs require a large measure of variety in local government. It bases its entire philosophy on the ability of people to govern themselves. Centralized government, in contrast, rests on the assumption that the people are incapable of self-government and that local differences, like the rights of minorities, must give way to what the leaders conceive to be the interests of the nation as a whole. It then becomes the duty of states and local communities to do as the central government directs, regardless of the wishes of the people of the locality. Federalism is rooted in self-reliance and cooperation. Centralization accepts dependence as inevitable. Under a federal system men and localities have a voice in their own government. Under a central system, they do as they are told.

VIII

REPRESENTATIVE GOVERNMENT TRANSFORMED

IF THE delegates to the Federal Convention of 1787 were to come back today, they would hardly recognize their handiwork.

Where they planned that the states should remain all-powerful in their own territories, the Federal government is now virtually supreme throughout the land. Where they had restricted the sphere of the Federal government to the bare functions of protection and the regulation of interstate commerce, the government is now in the banking and insurance business, regulates wages and hours of work, manufactures and distributes power, controls agricultural output, contributes to education, supervises the marketing of securities, dominates the nation's credit structure, and is engaged in countless activities undreamed of by the founders.

Where they had provided that laws should be drawn up, debated and passed by Congress, and approved or vetoed by the President, they would find a President having bills drawn up in his own office by his own assistants, and forcing Congress to pass these bills, often unchanged, and even unread. Where they had intended that each branch of the government should serve as a check on the others, they would find a large number of independent commissions whose acts not only are unchecked by the existing three branches, but some of which may not even be reviewed on appeal. Where they had made the selection of the President a process removed from popular clamor, they would find the President, in effect, chosen by popular vote. Where they had expected the Senate to be composed of elder statesmen chosen by the state legislatures, they would find that body made up of six-year Congressmen chosen directly by the people. Where they had believed that the suffrage would be restricted to men of property and intelligence, they would find that nearly everyone—Negroes excepted—over twenty-one years of age, not actually in jail or in an asylum, can vote, regardless of intelligence or fitness.

Far from remaining in the horse-and-buggy stage, the government has shown amazing elasticity and adaptability. The Constitution itself, despite the charge that it has created a system which is too rigid, has been freely amended. Not even the intentionally difficult combination of majorities in Congress and the states required to change the Constitution has blocked the amending process when the demand has been nationwide and powerful. In the first fifteen years of the Federal government's life, the Constitution was amended no less than twelve times. Between 1913 and 1933 six amendments were passed. Nothing is further from the truth than the assertion that the Constitution has been a straitjacket and has held the country back by imposing an unchanged and unchangeable governmental form designed for a pioneer people living in a primitive economic society—a form thus necessarily unsuited to a modern, highly industrialized state.

All three branches of the government have contributed to the process of change and modernization. The Congress, by the passage of laws extending the powers of the Federal government, has been an even greater factor in altering the governmental structure than have most of the Constitutional amendments. The courts, by interpreting the Constitution and laws when these have been questioned, have materially affected the government's development. The President, by framing policies calling for new instruments of power to be placed in his hands, and by facilitating, through executive orders, the growth of the administrative branch of the government, has, particularly in recent years, done much to make the Federal executive the dominant branch of the government. Finally, such extra-governmental organizations as political parties, and such factors as precedents, customs and traditions, have become constantly more important in the actual functioning—and hence in the growth and changes—of government.

The two-party system is now so deeply imbedded in the operation of the American government that it is hard to realize that the founders not only failed completely to reckon with it, but apparently believed that they could keep parties out of American political life altogether. How this could have been more than a hope on their part is not clear, for the founders had had wide experience in state and colonial politics and knew English history well. They must have known that His Majesty's Opposition was almost as important as His Majesty's Government in England, and that in any state there would surely be struggles on the part of the "outs" to replace the "ins." It can only be because they themselves buried their disagreements for the greater good of the whole that they assumed that the men who made up the government they proposed would also bury their differences and would serve their country, not a mere faction.

It was largely to create a government that was national, not factional, that President Washington brought into his cabinet such different men as Alexander Hamilton and Thomas Jefferson. But this move, instead of preventing the formation of parties, led to their creation. Personally antagonistic and differing fundamentally in political philosophy, Hamilton and Jefferson precipitated the first two political parties in the United States. Hamilton, native of the West Indian island of Nevis, lacked the sense of state loyalty. By inclination as well as by process of reasoning he was a nationalist. Jefferson, although author of the famous Declaration of Independence, was, in those days, primarily a Virginian. Thus, at the outset, the advocates of Nationalism and of States' Rights found their champions. But this was not the only difference between these men. Hamilton believed in a government by the best people for the masses. Jefferson believed that the masses should be permitted to govern themselves. Hamilton's philosophy might be termed impatient paternalism. Jefferson was the apostle of easy-going individualism. Hamilton wanted a strong, efficient government. Jefferson wanted as little government as possible. Hamilton thought almost entirely in terms of the concrete. Jefferson loved theories. One had a passion for facts, the other for words. Hamilton's outstanding trait was candor. Jefferson's was deviousness.

Out of the factions that surrounded these two figures came the party split that led, in 1800, to the election of Jefferson to the Presidency. We are less concerned here with the fact that, once in office, Jefferson turned nationalist and belied the dire prophecies of the Hamiltonian faction that the government would collapse under his mobocratic leadership, than we are with the fact that the spoils system, which was to do so much damage in American politics, was already in evidence at this early date. To Andrew Jackson is usually given the discredit of having fathered the spoils system. The truth is that John Adams and Jefferson had pointed the way. No candid student of political history can doubt that President Adams' last-minute appointments to numerous Federal offices—including that of John Marshall to be Chief Justice of the Supreme Court—were made for political purposes—just as Jefferson's attempts to "turn the rascals out" were political. The system thus inaugurated grew and flourished as an ugly excrescence on the body politic for nearly a century. Grover Cleveland was the first President to grapple with this evil courageously. He appointed the Civil Service Commission in 1883, and the first steps were then taken to place Federal office-holders on a merit system.

The civil service movement, in the half century since its inauguration, has not succeeded in breaking the hold of the political parties on the selection of the agents of government in nation and states. Today the party leaders still name all candidates, Federal, state and local, for elective offices, and virtually dictate to the President, the state governors and the mayors whom they shall nominate for all appointive offices under their jurisdiction. To this extent, the party leaders determine the personnel of government. They choose. The people only ratify or reject. And yet political parties are not mentioned—and not even implied—in the Federal Constitution.

In theory the political parties represent the voters at large. In fact, as shown in Chapter III, each party is dominated by a little handful of professional politicians. Their standards and reactions have already been described. The usual indifference of the voters makes it easy for the party bosses to run the country. When, as often happened, the bosses were crooks, the government itself was corrupt. The readiness of small politicians to "do favors" for big business—in return for a consideration—is as much responsible for the unholy alliance between crooked business and politics as is the readiness of crooked business to pay for favors received. The taker of a bribe is no less open to blame than he who offers the bribe.

As a result of the development of actual government in America the existence of two fairly evenly balanced political parties has become indispensable to the practical working of the system. When the size of a majority becomes too great the system ceases to function properly. This is especially true if one party not only controls the Presidency but has a large majority of both houses of Congress. Its tendency then is to ride roughshod over the minority. It is so insolent in its strength that it rejects criticism, however sound, and acts impetuously, contemptuously and usually domineeringly. This paralyzes one of the chief functions of Congress, which is to serve as a place for discussion—for the airing of opinions and the consideration of conflicting views. The value of frank and open debate in Congress or Parliament is to make the popular wishes known, and, incidentally, to avoid possible mistakes in desired legislation by pointing out helpful modifications of proposed measures. A minority party almost as strong as the majority not only is better able to defend the proper interests of the minority but works as a salutary check on the natural tendency of a majority to be arbitrary. When the parties are fairly evenly divided the majority has to pay heed to the minority. But when the minority is insignificant the majority does as it pleases, unchecked and unrestrained.

One of the evil consequences of this is that opposition becomes futile because it is so completely ineffective. The legislative branch of the government then ceases to function as it was intended. Instead of serving as a deliberative representative body it becomes a mere board of ratification. Why should the members of Congress pay attention to the measures for which they vote when they know that debate or criticism is futile, and that even modification is impossible because the Administration leaders are determined to jam through laws which the White House has placed on a list of so-called "must" legislation?

An extreme instance of this was pointed out in 1935 by Representative James W. Wadsworth, Jr., of New York, who remarked that during the discussion of one of the most important measures, only 35 of the 435 members of Congress were present on the floor. The reason for this insignificant attendance was that the members, whether present or not, knew that the Administration's forces were so strong that the bill would be passed as drafted in the White House without any change. They did not, under the circumstances, deem it worth while to waste their time on the floor of the House. That such a procedure is a mockery of representative government and a travesty of the intentions of the Constitution is obvious.

Not only does a big majority negate in this manner the effective working of constitutional government, but the danger exists that such a majority will be so subservient to the wishes of the party leaders that the administration in power can establish a kind of party dictation which overrides the American constitutional system.

It is, of course, obvious that a certain amount of direction and control is indispensable in any political organization which is to function effectively. The usual practice has been for party members to exercise their right of judgment and to participate in party councils and help shape party policies. Ordinarily they agree to support the actions determined by the majority of their party in caucus. Under the "mandate" theory, however, party members are expected to carry out the orders of the party leader—*i.e.*, the President—and to accept the doctrine that the overwhelming size of the vote cast for a President is a blanket endorsement by the nation, empowering the President to put into effect any policies which he believes desirable.

That such an interpretation is welcomed by the close friends and advisers of a President who has enormous

127

personal popularity, is understandable. But when the strong political pressure of the Presidency is used to force his party followers in Congress to enact all the laws which he wants, Presidential government displaces Congressional government, and Congress becomes superfluous.

The importance of this new development needs particular emphasis. If allowed to grow unchecked it may turn out to be revolutionary—in a most reactionary sense. While "mandate" government is only possible under an overwhelming party majority, the whole concept of a "mandate," as well as the manner of its application, is subversive of the principles as well as the forms of the American system. It is an open endorsement of purely personal government—of giving the ruler a free hand to do what he wants. By making Congress subservient to the President it substitutes the will of one man for the will of the Representatives. It takes the lawmaking powers from Congress, which was created to exercise them, and places them in the hands of the executive. Thus one of the basic checks is removed which was embodied in the Constitution for the purpose of preventing the kind of concentration of power now sought by the advocates of the "mandate" theory.

A good argument for Presidential government of the mandate type can be made—just as a defense can be established for Fascism or Hitlerism. But the system is the negation of that established in the American Constitution. Law-making was deliberately reserved to a body of men elected directly by the people. It was considered —as it should be—the function of the many, not of the few. To the President was assigned the duty of executing such laws as Congress might pass. To be sure, the President was given the right to recommend legislation. But it was not intended that he should draft bills—let alone use a strongly organized political machine for the purpose of jamming them through Congress.

There has been, of course, a constant rivalry between Congress and the President ever since the days of Washington. Each has endeavored to encroach on the powers of the other—with varying success. But Congress—and more particularly the House of Representatives—has been regarded by champions of democracy ever since 1787 as the real bulwark of democracy because of its powers to make and to change laws and to raise and spend money. Congressional government has been, in fact, the basis of the American system. The House has been the most truly representative body. It has come closest to furnishing a government which is genuinely of the people. When Congress becomes little more than a rubber stamp Congressional government—which means popular government—ceases to exist.

The trend toward Presidential government has been increasingly rapid during the last three decades. It is a natural—and probably logical—outgrowth of the transformation of the Federal government into a central government which has proceeded almost unhindered since the Civil War. Prior to that conflict, the tendency, as explained in Chapter VII, was already in evidence, but it had been held in check by the strength of the states' rights movement. Centralization actually began when President Washington took Alexander Hamilton into his first cabinet. It was furthered by John Marshall as Chief Justice of the Supreme Court. It received valiant support from three Democrats—Thomas Jefferson, Andrew Jackson and Franklin D. Roosevelt. Three other Presidents, two Democrats—Grover Cleveland and Woodrow Wilson—and one Republican—Theodore Roosevelt—likewise helped the process. Today—1938—it is riding roughshod over all obstacles. Each new extension of the central power leads to another, and those who advocate more power are actively propagandizing not only against the checks which Congress and the courts may still place on the President, but against the very existence of the states as independent, sovereign units.

The framers, as I have already explained, were confident that the states would hold the Federal government in check. But the states have been powerless to prevent the encroachments of the Federal government. This in itself has profoundly altered the original form of government, and has removed one of the barriers against concentration of power which the founders were so eager to see firmly and permanently established. Their intention, it must not be forgotten, was to divide power between the states and the Federal government. Deliberately they developed the Federal form, believing that this would preserve the states indestructibly in a union that would serve them all.

Another important check on the concentration of power disappeared when the 17th Amendment, providing for the direct election of United States Senators, was passed. The Senate, until 1913, was composed of men appointed by the state legislatures instead of, as at present, elected by popular vote. This method of indirect selection was deliberately adopted, as I have shown in Chapter VI, in the belief that it would make the Senators independent of the currents of passing popular passion to which the House was expected to be responsive. The contemporary records show clearly that the framers believed that a body so chosen would more effectively hold the House in check—that it would serve as a brake on unwise or impulsive legislation.

Today the Senators are as subject to the need of placating their constituents as are the Representatives. The Senate has become a secondary legislative chamber, adding little to the calibre of the government by superior intelligence or character, and being as susceptible as the House to popular clamor. The principal difference between the two bodies, apart from the length of service, is that the Senators look upon themselves as superior beings, and that where perhaps only half the

House of Representatives are potential Presidential candidates, each member of the Senate regards himself as the logical choice of his party to succeed the President.

The self-exaltation of the Senators has not prevented them from being as petty and partisan as members of the House. This has been particularly true in the work of the so-called Senatorial investigating committees. Many of these have held hearings conducted on the principle that witnesses are knaves or public enemies who may be insulted and browbeaten with impunity for the delectation of the public. The notorious Black investigating committee did not hesitate to seize secretly the files of all telegrams in and out of Washington between February and September, 1935, in order to try to "get something" on men whom they believed to have—but had not yet publicly charged with having — conducted lobbying activities in favor of the public utilities. That such seizure of private documents was a flagrant violation of the Constitution did not deter these gentlemen who had sworn by sacred oath to uphold that document. They were playing politics. Why, under the circumstances, allow the Constitution to hamper them?

The development of committees in the House has served the indispensable purpose of relieving the load on Congress as a whole of digesting the mass of bills brought before it in each session. The function of the committees is to study proposed bills, hold hearings upon them, redraft them or change them if necessary, and, if finally approved, to report the bills to the House for action. These committees, in fact, do most of the actual lawmaking. Congress as a whole rarely considers bills except to ratify—or reject—the work of the committees. Only when major political problems are involved is there general discussion of proposed laws.

It follows from such a procedure that the forming of these committees is most important. In practice this is done by the Speaker of the House. As the Speaker also has full authority to direct the order in which bills will be considered, his office has become one of the most important in the government. If he does not actually dictate the laws himself, he has a large influence in determining what laws shall be passed. Before the growth of Presidential government, it was not uncommon for a powerful Speaker to loom even larger in Washington than the President. While the founders planned that the House should be influential, they never expected that body to overshadow the Senate as it has, and they never dreamed that one Congressman, by being named Speaker, could virtually dominate the lawmaking process of the nation. Nor did they dream that a time would come when the Speaker was so subservient to the President that the laws would, in fact, be dictated by the White House secretariat.

Many of the changes in the American form of government that have occurred in the last one hundred and fifty years have been in response to structural needs as well as to political and economic developments in the nation. The extent of the changes shows the ready adaptability of this supposedly over-rigid Constitution. But when—as is now the case—the Federal government can tell every farmer what he may grow—and punish him for not doing as he is directed; when it can finance and organize the staging in public theatres of propagandistic plays written by men and women who would like to overthrow the government that feeds them; when it can establish and operate industries for the express purpose of "punishing" private business; when, in a thousand other ways it can help, hinder, control or coerce the people of the country in order to impose regulations devised by theorists and unwanted by most of the people, we have travelled a long distance from that simple and cautiously limited government which the founding fathers established a century and a half ago. In fact, representative government itself is now being challenged because its cumbersomeness hampers executive efficiency and because, under the new philosophy, efficiency is more to be desired than democracy.

IX

GOVERNMENT BY DECREE

THE GOVERNMENT which the founding fathers proposed was, as I have already indicated, a *representative* republic, in which the people delegated to *agents of their own choice* the authority to exercise for a *limited* period *specific* powers deliberately *checked* and *restricted* by a *written* constitution.

So important is this definition that it deserves not only repetition but elaboration.

The founders created a republic rather than a democracy because they felt that this system, in which representatives were to be chosen and empowered to speak for their constituents, was better adapted to an extensive territory and growing population than a democracy in which the people would retain a large measure of direct control over government. Thus from the beginning emphasis was laid on the representative character of the government, and it was intended that the elected representatives would not only be free to exercise their own judgment about matters of policy but would by training, education and character be fitted to act wisely and disinterestedly.

Independent as these representatives or agents were

to be, it was expressly provided that not only should they be chosen by the people from among the people, but that they should be answerable to the people and recallable by the people at the next election. The intention was that the representatives should be truly representative of the electorate that chose them, and, at the same time, that the electorate should be able to exercise a measure of control over the representatives by declining to re-elect them if the representatives did not do what the people wanted. In other words, the elected officers were to be responsible and accountable to their constituents.

The officers of the government were, with the exception of the judiciary, to serve for limited periods. By setting time limits it was planned to have frequent rotation and to make it difficult if not impossible for any group to entrench itself permanently in power. Thus it was hoped to allay the fear—so strong a century and a half ago—that a little clique of rulers could become all-powerful and self-perpetuating.

The powers granted to the various officials were specific. It was the intention of the framers that these powers should be so divided that no branch of the government could make itself supreme. The powers were defined by a written constitution so as to make doubly sure that they would not be abused and exceeded. The nature of the powers was clearly outlined. It remained only to fill in the details by the process of lawmaking.

That lawmaking would become immensely complicated was probably only inadequately sensed by the framers. Their ideal was a government that would leave to individuals the largest possible measure of personal initiative. Certainly they never dreamed that the Federal government would embark on extensive programs of regulating countless business and economic activities of its citizens. They could have had no idea of the difficult problems of administration as well as legislation that would arise as a result of government control of business. It is doubtful if even today more than a few members of Congress and a few students of government realize the extent of the knowledge, the judgment and the statesmanship which are required if laws regulating economic activities are to be wisely and soundly framed. Not only this, but the carrying out of these laws, whether they be good or bad, raises problems of administration and interpretation with vastly complicated repercussions.

It is not surprising that with the growth of the regulatory functions of the Federal government at least two new—and unforeseen—developments in the American system appeared. The first is the establishment of independent commissions and agencies, often spoken of as quasi-judicial bodies, the members of which are appointed by the President and hold office for long periods of years. The second is the wholesale resort, not only by these independent bodies but also by the executive branch of the government, to the use of executive orders, including departmental rules and regulations. Lawyers speak of these as "administrative law."

When the government began to enlarge its regulatory activities it became obvious that administrative agencies would have to be created to put the new regulative laws into effect. There was little coherence in the manner in which the new administrative powers were delegated. Congress at first attempted to place them in the hands of existing government agencies. But as the scope of the regulative powers was extended, the practice of creating new agencies arose. Sometimes these were under the direction of existing departments. Sometimes they were made independent commissions not responsible to the President and virtually free from Congressional control. The list of these commissions is long. The first—the Interstate Commerce Commission—was established in 1887. Today this and other commissions exercise supervisory and regulatory powers over many forms of business activities.

The creation of the independent establishments has raised two major questions: (1) whether, in view of the fact that much of their work is administrative, it is right to make these bodies altogether independent of the executive department of the government; and (2) whether they should be permitted to serve in a quasi-judicial capacity when their own acts or rulings are questioned.

Critics of the system contend that better administration could have been obtained by placing the administra-

tive functions of these bodies under one of the departments of the executive branch, leaving to a politically
independent or bi-partisan body the quasi-judicial
functions which some of them now exercise. Thus the
principle of separating executive from judicial functions would be observed. But the purpose of making the
commissions independent was to remove even their administrative functions from partisan influence. To place
the commissions in the government departments would
make them subservient to the Administration.

One of the worst features of the independent commissions is that their interpretative decisions and rules and
precedents have acquired the full force of law. It thus
results that extensive opportunities to amplify and par-
ticularize laws are now in the hands of small groups—
and sometimes individuals—in the administrative branch
of the government. Often these men exercise this legislative function without consultation, hearings, or adequate
discussion. Appeal from the rulings of these bodies is
complicated as well as expensive—in itself an evil.

To make matters worse, the quasi-judicial powers of
the independent commissions are often so exercised that
the commissioners act as the judges of the decisions and
orders of their own subordinates. Citizens affected by
these decisions cannot be blamed for feeling that they
cannot have a fair deal when the same body makes the
rules, enforces the rules, and passes on the rules when
they are questioned. It runs counter to American prin-

ciples to unite in the hands of one body legislative, executive, interpretative, judicial and punitive powers.

If the instances of this sort of activity were few they might be overlooked. But they take on added significance when the extent and rapidity of the growth of administrative law—of government by decree—in the United States is considered. A report of the President's Committee on Administrative Management published in 1937 states that there were then no fewer than 115 Federal agencies which, under 964 statutory provisions and 71 executive orders and proclamations, issued rules and regulations affecting the public—rules and regulations which, as I have already indicated, have the binding effect of law.

The right of Congress to delegate such power to amplify laws has been questioned in the courts, but the judicial practice has been to accept this delegation of power when it has been confined to the interpretation and execution of necessary and constitutional laws. As the President's Committee well put it, "the prerequisites of a valid delegation seem to be that Congress must itself have the power to regulate; must define the subject to be regulated; must declare a policy with respect to that subject and set up a standard or criterion for executive action; must require a finding, at least in contingent legislation; and must delegate rule-making powers to public officials and not to private persons." It is only when blanket powers have been granted that, as in the famous

Schechter case invalidating the N. R. A., the Supreme Court has held that Congress has exceeded its constitutional limits by surrendering the lawmaking power to the President. It was against this sort of "delegation running riot" that Mr. Justice Cardozo protested in his concurring opinion invalidating that act.

So long as administrative authorities are required to keep strictly within the bounds set for them by the law the danger of bureaucratic autocracy is small. But if Congress ever grants to the President or his subordinates what Professor William B. Munro calls a "wide-open authority" to make rules, the basic principle of the American system will, as he has pointed out, be overthrown.

With due respects to Dr. Munro's judgment, there are reasons to believe that the trend can become dangerous even before "wide-open authority" has been granted. The danger lies in the psychology—and the pathology—of commissions and of administrative law. Except where the commissions have been deliberately shorn of their powers by Congress, or restricted by the courts, their tendency is the same as that of all political bureaus —to reach out for more power, and to exercise their power with greater impatience of restraint as they feel themselves more securely entrenched as indispensable cogs of the government machinery. It is one thing to require by law that administrative authorities shall keep within the bounds set for them by Congress. But it is quite another to make certain that these authorities will

141

act wisely, fairly and justly. Most of the officials, high and low, who make up the personnel of these bodies, have been chosen for political reasons, often with little regard to their fitness. Many of them develop the defensive arrogance of small minds entrusted with large authority. When their decisions, rulings or acts are questioned by any one affected by them, they are tempted to justify and uphold themselves with a stubborn disregard of the rights of mere citizens.

This is particularly likely to happen when the rule-making authorities know that appeal from their decisions to the courts or other disinterested agencies is hard. Bureaucrats have an apparently irresistible tendency under such circumstances to become more pig-headed. The development of administrative law may thus lead toward an ever larger resort to the use of irresponsible authority, and hence to ever greater emphasis on the individual bureaucrat's prejudices and whims, instead of on a fair enforcement of the law.

In all consideration of the cognate subjects of commissions and of administrative law it is essential to distinguish between agencies which, like the Civil Service Commission and the office of the Comptroller General, were established to control and improve the functioning of government machinery, and those which, like the Interstate Commerce Commission, and various similar bodies, serve to regulate the conduct of business by individuals and corporations. Many of the same arguments that have been marshalled against one type may be used in favor of the other.

Against the independent commissions that control activities of individuals and corporations such as railroads, broadcasting companies, etc., for example, as I have already indicated, the charge is made that they violate the fundamental concept of separation of powers. They combine in themselves powers of legislation, administration and adjudication virtually unchecked and uncontrolled by any of the three branches of government. Their very independence is thus held against them.

In contrast, those bodies, like the office of the Comptroller General and the Civil Service Commission, which deal exclusively with public officials (and, in the case of the Civil Service Commission, with candidates for public office) have much to gain by being made—and maintained—entirely independent. Their purpose is to exercise a check on government employees, high and low. The very fact that they have been to date—1938—free from interference by the executive and by Congress, and that appeals have not been taken from them to the courts, except in rare instances, has given them strength and made their work more efficient.

The reason for this is obvious. As they deal entirely with the acts of government officials, and as many of these officials are professional politicians who can bring political pressure to bear, it follows that any man whose accounts are questioned, or whose promotion is denied, would be sure to mobilize all the political "pull" at his disposal if the Comptroller General's office or the Civil Service Commission were subject to Presidential or Congressional pressure. To resist this pressure it is indispensable that these two bodies be absolutely independent. There is significance in the fact that the office of the Comptroller General, whose powers have been much more autocratic than those of the Civil Service Commission, was more effective—and aroused more bitter hatred on the part of the professional politicians—than did the more docile Civil Service Commission. Appeal by government agents from the Comptroller General's decisions was virtually impossible short of a special act of Congress. Not a cent of government money could be spent without his approval, and if disbursed in defiance of his disapproval it became a charge on the disbursing officer. To spendthrift politicians he was thus a curse.

The Comptroller General was, without doubt, the most unpopular officer in the Federal government ever since the post was created in 1921. Politicians feared him. Bureaucrats had to put up with rulings of his office which seemed to them petty as well as unreasonable. Persons who wished to see government funds used for all manner of purposes resented with particularly acute bitterness his insistence on sticking to the letter of the law. In 1933, a virulent campaign to discredit the Comptroller General was started, and one of the major tenets of the governmental reorganization proposal advocated by

President Franklin D. Roosevelt was to abolish the office of the Comptroller General and substitute in its place an auditor general.

The attacks on the Comptroller General were centered on his powers to deny in advance expenditures of money. This, technically termed the power of "control," made him, so the opponents of the office claimed, a virtual dictator of policy as well as of expenditures, for the simple reason that many policies rest on expenditures, and the power to curtail these expenditures implies the power to paralyze the policies. What the critics advocated, therefore, was that there should be no independent officer required to pass on expenses in advance and authorized to disallow expenses without appeal. Instead they wanted only a post-audit—the locking of the financial stable after the horses had got away.

That such a solution appeals to the politically minded is obvious. It removes a check on public spending. It is much more convenient for the politicians and reformers to be unhampered in the use of public money until after it has been paid out, when they need only submit to an audit. In practical politics such an audit can hold little terror for the disbursing officer, as the money is gone and nothing can be done about it.

The commonest charge against the first Comptroller General, John R. McCarl, who held his office for fifteen years, was made with as much vehemence by Republicans as by Democrats—that he was arbitrary. This is true in so far as it means that he insisted on making his own interpretations of the laws. But from beginning to end he was guided by a strict construction of the law and tried to make it very plain in advance how his office interpreted specific provisions of particular acts appropriating money. To the extent that his decisions were final and that he was completely independent, his use of power often seemed to those under him to be high-handed —as I can testify from two and a half years' experience as a disbursing officer in the Federal government in the days of Comptroller General McCarl. But no one acquainted with government administration and aware of the pressing need for the elimination of waste and the practice of rigid economy would question the fact that the mere existence of such a "watchdog" is of inestimable value because of the realization that his rulings must be obeyed and cannot be appealed. Some such ironclad control is essential if government spending is not to be abused. Control cannot be truly effective if exercised through a post-audit by a political officer subservient to the President.

Fully as dangerous as the elimination of the Comptroller General is the recent innovation in Congress of voting large lump sum appropriations to be spent by the President as he sees fit, without any check or restraint by Congress. This is a direct reversal of the custom of a century, during which time Congress, charged by the Constitution with the power of raising and appropriating money, has always clearly and precisely earmarked the exact purposes for which the appropriated money could be spent. Persistently, before 1933, Congress declined to vote blanket sums in times of peace, conscious that appropriations of this sort place in the hands of the spending authorities—which means the executive branch of the government—enormous powers which the Constitution did not intend that branch to have.

Defenders of the practice have asserted that so long as Congress retains the right to refuse appropriations it does not surrender control of the spending power. This is a legalistic rather than a realistic interpretation. Technically it is correct. But, in practice, when Congress authorizes the spending of large sums and leaves the purposes as well as the details entirely in the hands of the executive, it is passing over to the President the real control of the use of that money. It then becomes the right of the President, not Congress, to say how and for what the money shall be spent. In so doing Congress gives the President the vast influence and power of patronage inherent in the distribution of billions of dollars—influence rarely before exceeded in scope and extent by any ruler of any country.

This is the kind of absolute power dear to the hearts of arbitrary rulers. They have always sought to obtain as large sums as possible from their people—and to avoid all restrictions on how the funds should be spent. Parliaments, on the other hand, have constantly struggled to limit the executive's spending power—whether he be King or President—and to hold the control of spending in the hands of the representatives of the people. As far back as ancient Rome it was a well-recognized principle that the control of the purse implies the control of public power.

In a democracy this principle is just as applicable as in a monarchy or an autocracy. Only the technique of control differs. Kings have sought money to maintain or enhance their prestige and power. In a democracy perpetuation in office rests on obtaining a majority of the votes. It follows, therefore, that if millions of voters can be placed on the government payroll it is possible to build up an enormous army of supporters who can be counted upon not to bite the hand that feeds them. Public funds are so used as to give to millions of voters a personal financial interest in keeping the Administration in power. The warning, as each election approaches, that the opposition, if it wins, will cut down relief payments and abolish all subsidies to farmers and other groups, is simply another way of saying: "Vote for us and we will support you." In plain English, the relief rolls and farm subsidies give whatever party happens to be in office millions of "heelers" who can be depended upon to keep that party in power.

As in all these problems everything comes back to politics—and hence to questions of personalities. Leaving a large amount of discretion about the spending of public funds in the hands of a President who is all-wise as well as truly benevolent can be defended on the score of efficiency. But who would defend such a grant if the money were to be spent by a weak President with bad advisers?

It is precisely because the framers of the Constitution, themselves wise in their understanding of practical politics and steeped in the lessons of history, realized that the personal equation plays such a large part for good or evil in government, that they sought to devise methods of controlling the possible acts of public officials by constitutional and legal restraints. The power of raising and appropriating money was deliberately lodged in the hands of Congress because this power was by implication so great that the framers declined to trust it to a single man. As a matter of fact, in American practice it has become abundantly clear that even the detailed control over appropriations worked out by Congress is not enough to prevent foolish spending.

The point at issue here, however, is not whether funds are well or unwisely spent, but rather, where the power which the free use of public funds gives to those authorized to make the expenditures should reside. The choice lies between Congress and the President. In this case the old adage about safety in numbers applies. While Congress can abuse the control of the purse—and has done so, as witness the soldiers' bonus—it is obvious that to enable a President and his political henchmen to spend unearmarked funds to suit themselves places upon a little group of political leaders an almost irresistible temptation to use these funds for political objectives. In Congress there are at least a few reciprocal checks on spending. A President, *per contra,* need feel no embarrassment about disposing of public funds as he wishes. If he is criticized he can always blame someone else.

It does not follow that such funds are used unethically in the sense of direct bribery of the voters. Expenditures of large sums of government money in a particular district can be presented to the voters as something of vital importance to the district's welfare. By constantly telling the residents of the district that they have gained from the money which the party in power obtained for them, the voters can easily be persuaded that their salvation lies in re-electing the party in office.

The practice of appropriating unearmarked sums for the use of the President is a manifestation in the United States of the world-wide trend toward the concentration of power in the hands of the executive. The blanket vote of appropriations is one of the methods by which Presidential government is being entrenched at the expense of Congressional government. Whether this is what those who vote the money intend, or whether it is part of a conscious plan of a little group of Presidential advisers, is beside the point. What counts is the fact that the surrender by Congress of the control over spending constitutes a change in the traditional methods of procedure under the American system which is but one of many that have been breaking down the balanced machinery originally designed to make it impossible for any branch of the government—let alone for any single individual in the government—to grasp most of the effective powers of government.

That the danger of such concentration was foreseen by George Washington is clear from his famous "Farewell Address." "It is important," he warned his countrymen in 1796, "that the habits of thinking in a free country should inspire caution, in those intrusted with its administration, to confine themselves within their respective constitutional spheres, avoiding in the exercise of the powers of one department to encroach upon another. The spirit of encroachment tends to consolidate the powers of all departments in one, and thus to create, whatever the form of government, a real despotism. A just estimate of that love of power, and proneness to abuse it, which predominates in the human heart, is sufficient to satisfy us of the truth of this position. The necessity of reciprocal checks in the exercise of political power, by dividing and distributing it into different depositories, and constituting each the Guardian of the Public Weal against invasions by the others, has been evinced by experiments ancient and modern; some of them in our country and under our own eyes. To preserve them must be as necessary as to institute them. If, in the opinion of the people, the distribution or modification of the constitutional powers be in any particular

151

wrong, let it be corrected by an amendment in the way which the Constitution designates. But let there be no change by usurpation; for, though this, in one instance, may be the instrument of good, it is the customary weapon by which free governments are destroyed."

X

UNCLE SAM, SPENDTHRIFT

POLITICIANS and reformers are making a spendthrift out of Uncle Sam. The politicians favor spending because they expect to be able to divert public funds to their own districts, often to the profit of their relatives and friends. The reformers, while opposed to the use of money for local political purposes, favor increases in the responsibilities and activities of government which involve large expenditures.

Few people seem to realize the elemental principle that the more services government performs the more government costs. Failure to understand this rests on two fallacies. The first is the assumption that because the public does not pay directly for most of the services it receives from government these services are performed without expense to any one. The second is that as money is issued by government, it follows that government's wealth is unlimited, and that therefore, even if government spends freely, it is merely tapping an inexhaustible supply of funds. Should government happen to run short of money all it need do is to print—or mint—more.

The truth is, of course, that even though the public does not pay cash directly for most services performed

153

by government officials, these men draw their salaries from funds obtained by the government through taxation. As taxes comes out of the pockets of the people—all the people—the cost of government is paid for by the people.

A large bureaucracy means a large payroll. The larger the bureaucracy the larger the payroll. The larger the payroll the larger the tax bill. As government is, by its very nature, clumsy and inefficient, the more services government attempts to perform the more it has to spend for overhead, and the larger the number of employees—which means the higher is the nation's tax bill.

If government could create money there would be no need of taxes. The problem of governing would be vastly simplified, as government could turn out all the money it needed to pay as many men and women as might be required to carry on the manifold functions of administration. But government does not create a single dollar. It does not manufacture money. The bills and coins which it has a monopoly of producing are merely measures of value which are accepted as such by the people at large. The prime function of money is to serve as a standardized gauge with which to measure goods and services that men buy and sell. In America we call this measure the dollar. In England they call their measure the pound. In order that our dollar might be anchored to something tangible and so be more or less unchangeable it was long provided by law that each dollar represented a fixed quantity of gold held in the public treasury. Before 1933 it took twenty dollars to buy an ounce of gold. Since 1933 the government has decreed that it requires thirty-five dollars to buy an ounce of gold. The change in value came by government fiat. Government can at will declare a new value for the dollar— or even adopt a new kind of currency based on carrots or pigs instead of gold.

The complicated and much debated intricacies of currency, gold standards, the silver question and credit control do not here concern us. The essential point is that government does not make money but only fixes its arbitrary value as a medium of exchange. The entire income of the government comes out of the people's pockets. Even the tons of gold and silver which the Treasury now holds in its vaults were paid for with the taxpayers'—or the lenders'—savings. In other words, all the gold and silver that the government owns, like all the money that the government spends, comes from the taxpayers or from the men and women who have bought government bonds and notes. To be sure, in 1933, the government confiscated all gold coin and bullion not already in the Treasury vaults. But this, which was described by a dissenting opinion of the Supreme Court as a form of robbery, was merely another method by which government took from its people the sums which government wished to spend.

Government's regular source of revenue is from taxes. Because people are by nature reluctant to pay taxes politicians have concentrated on obtaining taxes as painlessly as possible. The two favorite methods have been the use of indirect taxation—of taxes which are scarcely perceived because they are hidden or passed on so that they form part of the price of an article that is bought—and taxation of politically helpless minorities.

Aristotle, as I have shown in Chapter III, was one of the first to point out the political advantages of "soaking the rich." In recent years American politicians have followed his advice eagerly—and successfully. In ancient Athens demagogues blamed the rich for all the troubles of the times, and when popular resentment against the rich had been properly whipped up, heavy taxes and fines were imposed upon them. In America today the very rich are so few that they are politically helpless. No one champions their right to just treatment. On the contrary, to "soak the rich" is fair game, and the politicians spend hours thinking of ways of forcing the rich to pay for the cost of government—and the politicians.

Today two principles are well established: that taxes should be levied in accordance with ability to pay; and that from everyone who earns more than $100 a month should be extracted as much as he can be deceived into giving up. The income tax has been reserved for men of wealth. Indirect taxes are paid by the masses as well as by the wealthy. An income tax is easy to levy and collect and can be graded upward on a sliding scale until it becomes virtually confiscatory. Indirect taxes, on the other hand, can be so neatly hidden that the people who pay them can be fooled into thinking that not they but the reviled leaders of big business are in reality paying for them.

The trouble is that all efforts to place taxation on an honest basis—to bring it out in the open—are vigorously fought by the politicians of both parties. These gentlemen are interested in spending—not in saving. Their constant worry is that the source of the funds which they spend may dry up. Their efforts to devise hidden taxes are motivated by their fear that if ever the voters realize how much of the voters' own income goes for taxes they will raise such an uproar that the laws will have to be modified and that the sums at the disposal of the politicians will be reduced. It has even been expressly forbidden in some of the recent tax laws to advertise the amount which a purchaser pays in taxes on certain articles of consumption. The purpose is, of course, obvious—to hide from the consumers the fact that they are paying these particular taxes, lest the public, when finally it understands how it is being mulcted, will force the repeal of these and other tax laws.

How these indirect taxes pile up may be judged from studies made by various industrial producers to determine the accumulation of taxes on their products, from the time the raw material is produced until it is processed, distributed and retailed.

On each loaf of bread, for example, a total of 53 different taxes, national, state and local, are paid. These include taxes paid by the farmer, the processor and the distributor. On a pair of shoes 126 different taxes are paid. There are 57 different taxes on a quart of milk, from the cow to the consumer, and 216 on gas and oil, from the well to the filling station. These taxes are, of course, all paid by the purchaser. The Federal government alone gets more from a package of cigarettes than the tobacco farmer, the cigarette manufacturer or the retailer.

The struggle between government and taxpayers has dulled many pages of history. Government—be it a king, a dictator, or a representative republic—is always in need of funds. Even when the power of taxation has finally been lodged in a popularly elected legislature the antagonism continues to exist. This is why taxpayers, if they have been able to exercise political pressure, have sought to limit the powers of government to tax, and why so long the doctrine was popular that there should be a direct relation between the payment of taxes and the right to vote. It is obvious that there are dangers as well as potential injustices in allowing those who do not pay taxes to say how the tax money should be spent. This is not so much a reflection on the character and abilities of the non-taxpayers as it is a realization that those who do not pay for the cost of government will be much more ready to spend government funds than will those who have to provide the funds. In other words, non-taxpayers are free public spenders because they are disposing of other people's money, not their own. The temptation is great for them to try to squeeze as much money as possible out of the taxpayers to pay for services which the non-taxpayers rather than the taxpayers, demand.

Unfortunately many politicians have the non-taxpayers' mentality. Until recently most politicians were, in fact, actually exempt from taxes on their government salaries. Because spending has always been popular as well as easy they have consistently increased spending. In bad times they justify it as a form of "pump priming." In good times they say they are putting in "much needed improvements." Thanks to them the cost of governments of all kinds in this country is now five times greater than it was in 1913.

It is only fair to point out that the tax problem of America must be considered as a whole, and that the amount of taxes collected by state and local governments as well as by the Federal government must be considered together. Tax collection is one of the few functions of government exercised by national, state and local governments alike. As the amount which the citizens can be made to disgorge is necessarily limited it is of concern to each type of government how much the others collect in taxes. While there is rivalry among them, the politicians are at least practical enough to realize that none of them may kill the public goose that lays the golden tax eggs unless all of them are to suffer. Even though the adage about honor among thieves does not apply to politicians levying taxes, it can at least be said that they respect each other's rights in their joint pursuit of the taxpayers.

Plausible estimates indicate that only about a third of the nation's taxes are sufficiently direct to be consciously noted by the payers. These include personal and corporate income taxes, property, gasoline and sales taxes. The bulk of the other taxes are unperceived, unfelt and unrecognized. Yet the appalling fact stands out that the tax bill of the nation for all types of government is about seventeen billion dollars for the year 1938, and it is doubtful if the total national income will be more than sixty billions. It follows, therefore, that already about a quarter of the nation's income goes to support government activities of all kinds.

Various attempts have been made to estimate the exact amount which the head of a family with a small income pays in taxes. The figures range from about ten to twenty percent. Even if fifteen percent be accepted as a fair average it means that each wage earner works nearly two months a year to pay for government activities. While it is true that in return for this he gets valuable present and potential services—the use of schools and roads, police and fire protection, and various other similar activities—it is also true that his work supports thousands of bureaucrats in semi-idleness on a salary level often higher than his own, and that many of the services performed for him by these bureaucrats are extravagant, wasteful and futile.

Two aspects of taxes are usually ignored. The first is that the more a family pays in taxes the less it can spend for goods of all kinds. The second is that the higher the taxes on business, the higher the prices of the articles which business produces. High taxes thus inevitably tend to lower the standards of living. It has already been made clear that, as ninety percent of the families in America live on small fixed incomes, their well-being is directly affected by the quantity of desired goods and services they can obtain for a fixed amount of dollars. When taxes are high the proportion of income left over after taxes have been paid is reduced. When, in addition, prices are high, the quantity of goods that can be bought with these remnants of dollars is smaller.

Because of the difficulty of extracting enough taxes, governments have resorted extensively to borrowing. This is much less painful for everyone than the pay-as-you-go system. The politicians don't have to worry about alienating their constituents by increasing taxes. The taxpayers don't have to set aside a larger part of their income for the politicians. The lenders—those who purchase the government bonds—feel certain of a secure return on their investments.

It is by no means true that all borrowing is bad. Much depends on the purpose for which the money is borrowed, and on conditions in the country when the loans are floated. To borrow money for permanent improvements from which the community or nation will derive long use is, in the main, justifiable, provided the carrying charge is not too heavy for the community to bear. But to borrow money for public works that are not needed, or that are much more costly than is necessary, or a large part of the cost of which is not only extravagant but is spent in graft, is unwarranted. Too much of the borrowing by states and municipalities has been unjustifiable—as has been the time-honored custom of erecting unnecessarily expensive post offices, court houses and Federal buildings of all kinds to please the Congressmen of a given district.

So also, money borrowed in emergencies like the great depression in order to permit government to function and government salaries to be paid during the temporary cessation of tax payments, is justifiable. The same may be said of money borrowed for relief in the midst of a depression. But to borrow money for running expenses or relief when the depression is over is as unsound as it is indefensible. This is the sort of borrowing that leads to disaster.

The general proposition may be laid down that in good times debts should be paid off, and in bad times they should be incurred. So also, in good times public works should be reduced to a minimum. In bad times they should be greatly increased. There should even be extensive planning for public works in good times, with provisions to start operations as quickly as normal business activities begin to decline sharply.

The Chairman of the Federal Reserve System, Mr. Marriner Eccles, indicated the correct policy when he remarked, in the course of testimony before a public hearing, that if the Republican administrations that followed President Wilson had cut down the national debt even faster than they did—they reduced it from about $26,000,000,000 to about $16,000,000,000—the Roosevelt administration would have found it easier to finance the depression. What he meant was that if the national debt can be reduced as rapidly as possible in good times the strain on the national credit in bad times will be much lighter.

The steady increase of the national debt since 1930, regardless of recoveries and recessions, has, of course, created a situation which, if a new and serious crisis like another world war or great depression comes, may well prove disastrous. No thoughtful person can consider the piling up of deficit upon deficit and the steady increase in government expenditures of all kinds in the last decade without realizing that the nation is heading toward a fatal calamity. Sooner or later the point will come when the government will have to resort to repudiation or to inflation. Either will produce a major financial crisis, perhaps attended by serious social uprisings. With repudiation or inflation the savings of 40,000,000 people would go up in smoke, and the life insurance—and social security insurance—policies of the masses would be worth little more than the paper on which they are written.

For none of the major problems of our times is a paper solution easier to postulate—and harder to put into effect—than for this problem of over-spending: Not only stop adding to the government's running expenses, but actually begin to cut them.

The difficulty lies in the human equations. Politicians, as repeatedly emphasized, take pride in spending—especially in getting benefits for their constituencies which are paid for by other taxpayers. For instance, a Congressman from Wyoming is delighted if he can have a new post office built by the Federal government with funds largely obtained from taxpayers outside his state. Representatives of the poorer farm states eagerly welcome the pouring into their districts of hundreds of millions of dollars of farm relief paid for in large part by the taxpayers in the Eastern cities and industrial centers.

Furthermore, the reduction of government spending nearly always implies removing men from the government payrolls. As many of these men are the protégés if not the actual relatives or friends of politicians, political pressure against taking them off the public payrolls is great. Every public job, actual or potential, which is eliminated means one less opportunity for politicians to purchase support for themselves or their party at public expense. So also, politicians hate to see any government contract—in force or proposed—halted, as contracts mean work in somebody's district, and rightly or wrongly, the political leaders in that district manage to take the credit for all government contracts within their territory. This work brings business to the district. Its cessation retards business, and may well throw non-political employees out of jobs.

It may thus be said that there is, in fact, a silent conspiracy among politicians not to reduce government spending. Each one proclaims his devotion to the principle of economy in general but opposes it when it affects his particular interests. As the conduct of a large political body like the House of Representatives or a state legislature—in which originate, respectively, all proposals for Federal and state expenditures—requires a lot of give and take, the custom has become firmly established that every Congressman or Assemblyman will vote for the other fellow's request for an appropriation so that the other fellow will return the compliment.

For this condition there is no remedy other than a taxpayers' strike. This means not that taxpayers should refuse to pay their taxes, but that they should serve notice on their representatives that if government spending is increased the representatives will be held responsible and will be voted out of office. The fear of defeat at the polls, not the fear of mere vocal disapproval, is the only thing that can bring a politician to heel. Let him once be convinced that if he does not reduce government expenditures he will be turned out of office, and he will sacrifice his political friends, and even his relatives, if to do so is the only way of saving his own skin. To them he will justify his course by saying that if he were to be forced out they would have to go anyway, whereas if he stays on he can at least watch for a new chance of putting them on the payroll again—poor consolation, to be sure, for those who get the ax, but at least better for the elective official than being himself beheaded.

The tax problem goes to the very roots of the entire relationship of men and government in America. The choice lies between more government activities and more spending on the one hand, and less government activities and less spending, on the other. If government is to reach out and not only perform all kinds of services formerly furnished by private initiative, but also to control and direct extensive economic activities, there is no way of escaping enormous increases in the tax burden. Government costs money. More government costs more money. The more money government spends the more it has to raise. Unless it resorts to inflation it has no alternative but to continue to increase taxes.

There is a limit, obviously, beyond which taxes cannot be increased. It is idle to pretend that all that is necessary in order to obtain more money for government to spend is to increase the national income—that delusive term given to a bureaucrat's guess as to the sum total of the earnings of the American people in any given year. There is no clear and easy way of increasing this national income. The trouble lies in the fact already stressed—that the greater the increase in taxes the less men have left to spend for their ordinary living. Furthermore, as indicated at the beginning of this chapter, higher taxes almost inevitably force a general raising of prices with the result that men can buy less with each dollar. There comes a point, finally, when the burden of paying for government is more than the people can—or will—bear. When that point is reached, civil strife is around the corner.

Those who call for more government activities have given little or no thought to the problem of how to pay for them. Their attitude is the same as that of one of the principal defenders of the Townsend plan who, when asked by a member of a Congressional committee how the money would be raised to finance the countless billions which that plan would cost, replied that that was up to Congress—that Congress, and not he or the advocates of the Townsend plan, was responsible for raising the nation's funds.

This is, of course, evading the issue. Government has only two alternatives—to increase taxes, or to reduce its activities. If it is to spend more it must somehow, somewhere, obtain the money it spends. When the limit to borrowing is reached the choice is, as already pointed out, between inflation or repudiation, on the one hand, and greatly increased taxation on the other. If, *per contra*, government is to stop spending more money it cannot embark on new and more costly measures of control, or on extensive public works and other undertakings—let alone pay large bounties to politically privileged groups, like the farmers, the legionaires and the voluntarily unemployed.

America must choose.

THE NEW REACTION

XI

THE CONTAGION OF COLLECTIVISM

COLLECTIVISM has become the creed of modern reformers. Each of its different sects is convinced that it alone has the key to the terrestrial paradise. They quarrel among themselves about the apparently conflicting doctrines that they preach, but they are as one in putting the interests of society and the state above the interests of the individual, and they are as one in their emphasis on carefully planned, well-directed governmental efforts to reach their goal. Organization and procedure are to them of fundamental importance. As they assume that men and women, unaided and undirected, are incapable of living their own lives so as to fit in with the needs of the new society, they believe that there should be a group of leaders empowered not only to plan but to supervise, direct, enforce and punish. In short, paternalism is the essence of collectivism.

Collectivist—or totalitarian—forms range from communism through the various types of state socialism to state-controlled capitalism and finally, to fascism. These forms, although alike in their emphasis on the state supreme, differ materially in their ultimate objectives and their philosophy. Communism, for example, is avowedly

171

in the interest of the proletariat—by which term the communists refer to the workers of all classes who sell their labor for wages. It seeks to overthrow the capitalist system and to abolish private ownership of property and the means of production. Fascism, on the other hand, is bitterly hostile to communism, and seeks to preserve private property and the capitalist system, albeit under strict control and regulation. Where communism wishes to create a class government of the workers, fascism seeks to maintain a class government designed to appeal to the middle and upper classes. Most of the varieties of state socialism in between these two extremes contemplate the expansion of government to take control of the principal businesses of a country. They wish to get rid of private capitalists and to socialize capital. Many of them plan the abolition of private ownership of land as well as of most income-yielding property.

Although the ultimate aim of communism is a classless society in which the role of the state shall become more or less superfluous, the communists in Russia, like the fascists and the nazis, have based their tactics on the forcible seizure of the machinery of government and the establishment of a dictatorship by a small group. The dictators under these different forms have taken unto themselves all the powers that they have believed necessary and expedient. They have suppressed opposition parties, they have silenced their critics, and they have killed their more dangerous enemies. Nationalism has been glorified by each dictator, and the responsibility of the party leaders to serve the nation—and hence the people—has been frankly accepted. Each dictator has rested his claim to rule on his promise to save his country in an emergency. The new machinery of government has been reinforced by a powerful nationalist propaganda to spread the new political gospel, and by an extensive campaign to enlist sympathy, support and converts abroad.

It is too early yet to appraise the full measure of accomplishment of these different authoritarian states. There seems little doubt that the Russian people of today enjoy numerous benefits that they did not have in the days of the Czars. The Italians and Germans may be happier than they were before the advent of Mussolini and Hitler. They have approved their own particular forms of dictatorship. But it does not follow that other nations would be equally benefited by the adoption of some sort of communist or fascist or national socialist government, or that resort to authoritarianism or collectivism is the only way in which the weaknesses of democracy and the parliamentary system can be overcome.

What concerns us here more than this sort of quasi-historical speculation is the fact that, due largely to the distrust and resentment against the established political and economic order which has been cumulative since the World War and the great depression, the people in most of the Western world are receptive to evangelical economic doctrines. The collectivist seed has fallen on fertile ground. Reinforcing the emotional response is the fact that a strong rational argument in favor of state control of the economic system can be made. This is based on the extent to which great corporate structures, cartels and trusts have modified the individualist basis of society that existed down to the middle of the nineteenth century, and have created in its stead a corporate society largely controlled and directed by a comparatively few financiers and industrialists. If, the argument runs, the mass of mankind must work for others, why is it not both logical and just to substitute for the private owners of capital a single owner, the state, which, instead of seeking profits, as do the economic royalists, would see to it that earnings were equitably distributed among the workers?

The doctrine has wide appeal. Any candid survey of the world on almost any day in the last twenty years cannot fail to give the impression that ours is an age of social insanity and economic injustice and cruelty. The fact that this age was preceded by the comparative calm, comfort and orderliness of the pre-war half century makes the present seem all the more intolerable. At the same time it inclines critics to overlook the fact that similar social and economic inequalities and blunders have been manifested throughout the ages.

The past existence of evil conditions is, of course, no justification for their present continuation. The fact

174

that other depressions have been—or seemed—as terrible as that following 1929, in no way alleviates the distress of our own times. But it is instructive to learn that men's minds seem to react in the same manner in the face of similar economic conditions—and to recall that the world has managed to pull itself out of other depressions, and has moved on to fresh economic gains.

The following extract, for example, might well have been written by Mark Sullivan in 1933. It comes, however, from the pen of Andrew D. White and was written more than fifty years ago about the reaction in France during the French Revolution: "In speeches, newspapers and pamphlets about this time [1792], we begin to find it declared that, after all, a depreciated currency is a blessing; that gold and silver form an unsatisfactory standard for measuring values; that it is a good thing to have a currency that will not go out of the country and which separates [this country] from other nations; that thus shall manufacturers be encouraged; that commerce with other nations may be a curse, and hindrance thereto may be a blessing; that the laws of political economy, however applicable in other times, are not applicable to this particular period, and however operative in other nations, are not now so in [this country]; that the ordinary rules of political economy are perhaps suited to the minions of despotism but not to the free and enlightened inhabitants of [this country]."

Here were inflation, devaluation, going off the gold

standard, economic nationalism and a general demand for a new deal because the rules of the old deal had failed, all rolled into one.

So also the comment of *Harper's Weekly* in the midst of the severe depression of 1857 has a modern sound. "It is a gloomy moment in history," the editor wrote. "Not for many years—not in the life-time of most men who read this paper—has there been so much grave and deep apprehension; never has the future seemed so incalculable as at this time. In our own country there is universal commercial prostration and panic and thousands of our poorest fellow-citizens are turned out against the approaching winter without employment, and without the prospect of employment.

"In France the political caldron seethes and bubbles with uncertainty; Russia hangs as usual like a cloud, dark and silent upon the horizon of Europe; while all the energies, resources, and influences of the British Empire are sorely tried, and are yet to be tried more sorely, in coping with the vast and deadly Indian insurrection, and with disturbed relations in China.

"Of our own troubles [in America] no man can see the end. If we are only to lose money and by painful poverty to be taught wisdom, no man need seriously despair. Yet the very haste to be rich, which is the occasion of this widespread calamity, has also tended to destroy the moral forces with which we are to resist and subdue the calamity!"

In retrospect the problems of those times seem trivial, especially when contrasted with the new and appalling problems which the world faces today. To our great-grandfathers, however, their problems appeared insurmountable and the forces that could deal with them seemed impotent. But solutions were finally found, whereas today the problems left by the World War and the great depression remain unsolved by those in power.

This is what lends special plausibility to the oft-repeated demand of the reformers for a clean sweep. Why not, they keep asking, accept the fact that the old order has failed? Why not make over the economic and political structure so as to benefit society as a whole, on the theory that what helps society helps the individuals who make it up? If abuses have arisen under the capitalist system, scrap it. If great corporations are too strong, make the government even stronger so that it can control them and make them behave. If great fortunes are an evil, abolish them. The world can—and must—be renovated so that rational, kindly human beings can live in it without too much anguish, and so that material want shall be abolished—as it surely can be in this age of potential plenty.

This is the great challenge to the liberals of the world. It is not enough for them to insist that collectivism is reaction, and that the kind of governmental control established in Soviet Russia or in Nazi Germany is the negation of all that the liberal movement has stood for

177

during two centuries. To say this is to indulge in mere historical hair splitting—a substitution of dialectics for constructive thought. On the liberals rests the clear duty of explaining what, if anything, they propose to do if they continue to fight the trend toward collectivism.

It is the special misfortune of the liberals that they are too honest—that they are unwilling to promise the moon. Study of history has made liberals doubt that collectivist plans and panaceas can work. They realize that there is little in governmental practice that has not been tried out in the past, and that only too often government has failed as an instrument of reform. Because they are unwilling to propose a golden age which they know they cannot bring into being they are at a great disadvantage in trying to combat collectivist propaganda, with its emphasis on leisure, ease and plenty for the masses. Nothing that the liberals can offer has the romantic appeal of the various kinds of panaceas put forward in the name of collectivism.

To make matters worse the liberals, when they are challenged by the facts—not alone by the taunts of the radicals—are forced to admit that many of the indictments against capitalism as it has operated are true, and when they are attacked for having no cure-all that they can offer with zeal and conviction, they have to plead guilty to the charge. In other words, they are made to seem mere stupid defenders of the existing order, lacking imagination, intelligence and sympathy.

It is because of the combination of circumstances that the challenge of collectivism is so successful. The western world is still under the hypnosis of "progress" and still firmly believes that new proposals, if put forward in the name of the greater good of the masses are, ipso facto, "progressive." The cult of novelty still has more adherents than the cult of experience, and every change is undiscriminatingly hailed as "progress." The collectivists of different kinds, therefore, have not hesitated to appropriate the label of "progress" to their movements. Their constant insistence that all who oppose them are Bourbons has blinded many good people to the fact that collectivism, or paternalism, or the totalitarian or authoritarian state—call it what you will—is fundamentally reactionary in that it seeks to return to government almost unlimited powers over the individual citizens of the state.

It may be that the world is ready to welcome the reaction that is being forced upon it. No less an authority than Benito Mussolini has insisted that, just because the nineteenth century was the century of socialism, liberalism and democracy, it does not follow that the twentieth century must also be the century of socialism, liberalism and democracy. "If the nineteenth century was the century of the individual (liberalism implies individualism)," he recently said, "we are free to believe that this [the twentieth] is the 'collective' century, and therefore the century of the State."

To Signor Mussolini liberalism is a sterile and destructive doctrine, destined to lead the world to ruin. Its failure explains, in his words, why all the political experiments of our day are anti-liberal. "It is supremely ridiculous," the Duce has said, "to endeavor on this account to put them [the new experiments] outside the pale of history, as though history were a preserve set aside for liberalism and its adepts; as though liberalism were the last word in civilization beyond which no one can go."

Many persons who are not fascists would agree with Mussolini's diagnosis. Already, in America as in England, many thoughtful persons sincerely question the soundness of the liberal articles of faith. They doubt the effectiveness of popular government—the true utility of universal suffrage, the practicability of selecting good men for administrative work by resort to the ballot.

Mussolini has no hesitation about openly attacking the entire system. "Fascism," he has explained, "is opposed to classical liberalism which arose as a reaction to absolutism and exhausted its historical function when the state became the expression of the conscience and will of the people. Liberalism denied the state in the name of the individual; fascism reasserts the rights of the state as expressing the real essence of the individual."

Here is a challenge to the political philosophy of the Western world—a frank repudiation of everything in which the American people have believed for a century and a half. "Anti-individualistic," Mussolini continues, "the fascist conception of life stresses the importance of the state and accepts the individual only in so far as his interests coincide with those of the state, which stands for the conscience and the universal will of man as an historic entity."

If this were the challenge of fascism alone, it could be ignored as a local aberration of the Italian people. But it expresses in blunt terms the underlying concept of communism and nazism as well as of fascism. The Russian and German experiments have exalted the state above the individual and have created forms of dictatorship as absolute as that of fascism, even if their spokesmen have not been quite as baldly anti-liberal as has Mussolini.

Against the spread of such ideas there are few effective barriers. Suppression, hard enough in a despotism, is impossible in a democracy. Censorship can be used to shape and guide emotions and to win support for those in power, but it is a flimsy shield against a compelling concept which has an overwhelming appeal. Censorship is essentially the tool of those who base their case on force —a weapon of aggression rather than of defense.

American democracy has been slow to recognize this, and has tried to silence and exclude the advocates of hostile doctrines. This negative policy too often has served to help, rather than stifle, the censored cause. It has won sympathy and interest for foolish agitators who otherwise would have been ignored. The English, in contrast, have allowed extremists to talk themselves hoarse, confident that the common sense of the English people would protect them from "dangerous thoughts."

In America the intolerance of groups which, like some of the self-styled patriotic agencies, have been eager to do all in their power to fight the collectivist enemies of democracy, has been so extreme that it has turned against them many of the people whose aid they want and need. To make their efforts even less effective, the very vehemence of their statements suggests that these self-styled patriots are uncertain whether the American system can stand on its own feet. Alarmed by the apparent indifference of the American people to American traditions they have mistaken this popular apathy for a basic weakness in the system itself. They have thus concentrated on trying to isolate the American people from alien propaganda, when what is needed is an effective and nationwide campaign of a positive character setting forth simply and clearly the inestimable advantages of the American system, and facing frankly the question of how it can be improved and strengthened.

To pretend that the American system is perfect is just as silly as to insist that it is outmoded. Like all governments it is clumsy and tends to lag behind economic changes. It can—and should be—modernized if the need for such modernization can be clearly established and if it can be shown that the proposed changes will achieve the desired purpose without sacrificing cherished safe-guards. The Constitution is, after all, resilient, pliable, responsive. Were it rigid it would long since have frozen upon the American nation a system devised for a totally different era, and the American people would be justified in experimenting with almost any alternative—including forms of collectivism.

XII

PLANNED ECONOMY

OF ALL the proposals for applying rationalized methods
to the solution of contemporary problems none is more
plausible than planned economy. It has a reassuring
ring. Everybody likes a plan—and conveniently forgets
that most plans do not work out as intended. The use
of the word "economy," though technical in the sense
of "political economy," suggests that the plan will not
be extravagant or difficult to put into effect.

And, in truth, on paper few plans seem more sensible
and simple. The fundamental idea is that there shall be
a balance between production and consumption—that
a nation shall produce only those goods which it can
itself consume or for which it has a sure market abroad;
and that it shall buy from abroad only those articles
which it cannot itself produce. It implies the planning
of national life in the interest of the nation as a whole.
It assumes that there is an ascertainable limit to a nation's capacity to consume and to the world's capacity
to absorb a nation's surplus. Production is to be adjusted to consumption. This means that those industries
and branches of agriculture which today produce too
much must reduce their production. Those which pro-

duce too little must either increase their output or must be supplemented by imports.

This is so reasonable that it seems presumptuous to question it. If production can be made to balance consumption—if the farmers and manufacturers can be assured a market for all their goods at profitable prices —most of the nation's economic problems could be easily solved. Here would be security of the best kind—security of employment for the workers, security of profits for the employers, security of income for the investors. There would be no more depressions or booms. Instead there would be balanced plenty—a perfect economic equilibrium, based on reason rather than greed, on forethought and coordination instead of on selfish competition.

So complete and perfect a solution of the nation's troubles cannot be lightly dismissed. If it can work it deserves the nation's solid support. If it is a delusion this fact should be made known.

Let us, therefore, examine it in detail.

To begin with, a planned economy involves a plan. A plan calls for a board of planners. The planners, faced with the task of planning the economic life of 130,000,-000 persons of different occupations, different origins, and living under different climatic and economic conditions, must be men of phenomenal intelligence. It is no exaggeration to say that a national economic planning board should include a Socrates, a Solomon, a J. P. Morgan, Sr., a Henry Ford, an Einstein, and a James

Aloysius Farley. These men would have to inform themselves in detail about the complete economic activities of the entire nation and devise a plan to improve them. The amount of information which they would have to assimilate, and the foresight and wisdom that they would have to use, stagger the imagination. They would have, furthermore, to be infallible.

After assembling and mastering the basic factual material about production the board would have to acquire a complete understanding of the nation's transportation problems and of existing and potential machinery of distribution. From this it would have to pass on to the study of the needs and wants of the consuming public, and of their spending habits and, of course, their individual incomes. Unless a completely accurate knowledge of consumption is obtained it would be impossible to adjust production correctly to consumption.

With all of this information thoroughly digested, the board would then have to ration production in all lines, assigning to every producer of each kind of article an exact quota. So also it would have to regulate consumption, for an increase or decrease in the planned consumption would throw the whole system out of balance.

On the face of it this sounds comparatively simple. But when it is realized that statistical material about at least ten million producers would have to be assembled —and collated with the buying habits of at least thirty million families—it becomes apparent that, quite apart

from the exercise of wisdom and fairness in making allotments, the mere task of assimilating the necessary information is beyond the capacities of the human brain.

Let us, however, for the sake of argument, assume that
a master plan has been worked out, and that it is wise
and adequate. Remains the task of putting it into effect.
This involves, in the first place, a vast new army of bureaucrats whose function will be to tell producers what
they are to be permitted to produce and to see that they
do not exceed their allotments. In the second place it implies vesting in these or other agents the necessary
powers to punish non-compliers.

The reason for this should be obvious. If a plan is
to be put into effect it means that the allotted quotas of
production must not be exceeded by authorized or un-
authorized producers. Only those allowed to grow wheat
may be permitted to grow wheat, and no one may raise
pigs unless he has an allotted pig quota. Any pig-
chisellers—or wheat, hog or potato bootleggers—must
be punishable by fine or imprisonment unless the whole
system is to break down.

But this is not all. As production is to be balanced to
consumption, and as the power of consumers to buy is
effected in large measure by the prices at which goods
sell, it is indispensable that the board of planners not
only be able to fix prices but to see that these prices are
maintained.

Those who advocate this sort of planning are not dis-

mayed by its rigidity, nor by the fact that it implies
government control over the entire economic activities
of the nation. Prof. R. G. Tugwell, writing on this subject in *The American Economic Review* in 1932 said,
"Planning will necessarily become a function of the Federal government; either that or the planning agency
will supersede that government . . . business will logi-
cally be required to disappear. This is not an overstate-
ment of emphasis; it is literally meant. The essence of
business is its free venture for profits in an unregulated
economy. Planning implies guidance of capital uses;
this would limit entrance into or expansion of operations.
Planning also implies adjustment of production to consumption; and there is no way of accomplishing this except through a control of prices and of profit margins.
. . . New industries will not just happen as the automobile industry did; they will have to be foreseen, to
be argued for, to seem probably desirable features
of the whole economy before they can be entered
upon."

Such a system implies, of course, that not only would
government have the power of setting the limits beyond
which men would not be permitted to produce, but that
it would find itself in the position of seeing that none of
the producers fell below their allotments. As the English
economist C. D. H. Cole put it in his sympathetic volume
entitled "Economic Planning," "there can be no real
planning without a planning authority empowered to

lay down what *shall be* as well as what *shall not be* produced."

What this means, in plain English, is a return to a form of economic slavery, with the single difference that instead of men being forced to work for their individual owners they will be forced to work for the state. Instead of carrying out the orders of their masters they will carry out the orders of the agents of the state. They will not even have the solace of the personal relationship that existed between masters and slaves before 1863—the owner's solicitude for the well-being of the slaves and their families.

So fantastic does all this sound as the second quarter of the twentieth century is drawing to a close that it would not merit the consideration of serious-minded men if the theory of planned economy were not, in fact, being put into practice on a large scale in Russia and Germany, and if there were not already on the American statute books numerous laws based on this philosophy and embodying these principles.

In Germany agriculture is now so completely planned that the farmers' actions are directed and closely supervised by government agents. These men visit every farm in Germany to see that the farmer brings in to the nazi marketing agency *all* that he produces—including milk, eggs, pigs and garden "truck." Fixed prices for each article are set by the government bureaucrats in Berlin. If a farmer wants to retain the use of even a pint of milk he must buy it back from the government agent to whom he delivered it. He is obliged to fertilize and sow his acres as directed by the government agents. If he fails to operate the farm as the supervisor believes it should be operated, the property can be confiscated by the government and the former owner can be forced to work his former farm as a servant of the government.

When the supply of breadstuffs began to run short in Germany in 1937, an edict was issued in July requisitioning all wheat and rye crops. Farmers were forced to deliver all of these crops that they produced, except just enough for their own families. If a farmer was caught feeding cereals to live stock he could be fined as much as $40,000.

Even in thoroughly disciplined Germany many farmers refuse to live up to the rigid quota system. As a result, there is much bootlegging of foodstuffs. It has been estimated that as much as one-third of all food produced is sold surreptitiously. The penalties for this illicit trade are severe—first, heavy fines, then imprisonment. With true German logic and efficiency bootlegging of foods on a large scale can even be punished by death. Thus is this portion of Germany's planned economy being put into effect—and the people continue to be undernourished.

In America the same principles have been applied—although less rigidly and arbitrarily. The American experiments with planned economy began with the logical procedure of reducing temporarily the output of certain crops of which there was a great oversupply due to the closing of European and domestic markets. The first controls applied to wheat, corn and hogs, tobacco and cotton. But almost at once unforeseen complications arose. When farmers agreed to reduce their customary acreage in one of these crops they naturally looked around for other productive uses for the land taken out of their usual crops. As, one after another, they turned to other crops, an oversupply of these new crops was soon threatened. Immediately those farmers whose livelihood had depended on these crops demanded that controls be extended so that farmers turning to new specialties would not force down prices and ruin the long established producers of these specialties.

The famous potato control act of 1935 epitomizes the whole movement. The act was passed in response to the demands of the potato growers of Maine and Idaho when, due to the shift to potatoes of many tobacco farmers and others whose crops were being controlled, the country was threatened with a great glut of potatoes. The potato control bill typified at once the logic and the absurdity of the entire system. It was logical in that it not only established quotas for every farmer producing more than five bushels of potatoes, but also provided a fine up to $1,000, or imprisonment up to a year, for any potato grower attempting to sell more than his quota. As if this were not enough it also provided a similar penalty for any one knowingly buying bootleg potatoes.

The reaction was almost instantaneous. Had the law not been repealed shortly, the country would probably have had a large army of potato martyrs—men and women eagerly defying the law by growing more than the permitted allotment of potatoes and insisting on going to jail if arrested.

The preambles of the early agricultural control acts state specifically that they were emergency measures. Today (March, 1938) new controls are being devised under new terminology, and it has become clear that the goal is as Professor Charles A. Beard said it was in 1934. In his study of the New Deal called "The Future Comes," he said of the farm control program that "the government has so penetrated the institutions and procedures of the industry, from the highest national groupings to the smallest local units throughout the land, as to gather into its hands absolute control over every act of production, processing, manufacturing and marketing of practically all agricultural and associated commodities. Within the framework of the land bank system, it has established a network of banks and credit institutions adequate to meet almost every conceivable need for agricultural finance and credit. The program affirms the determination of the Administration to organize agriculture from the soil to the market, which is a first essential step toward gearing agricultural productivity to effective consumptive capacity within the nation."

One of the greatest evils of piecemeal planning is that each control leads to further controls. The reason for this is that each control upsets established business practices, with the result that pressure groups demand still further restrictions. The original crop control bill extended control from production to distribution and thence to processing. It is shortly expected also to dominate marketing. Once started on this course the inevitable goal is government control of all economic activities. The more control the government exercises, the greater the difficulty of enforcement. This, in turn, makes it necessary to use compulsion, and compulsion means resort to the state-all-powerful. It stands to reason that a government that controls the economic life of the nation controls the personal lives of its citizens. Economic dictation—and this is of the very essence of economic planning—involves political dictation. If government is to tell men what they *may not* grow it soon comes to tell them what they *must* grow. When it tells them what they must grow and an individual refuses, it must force him to do as he is told. This means the end of personal freedom.

But there are at least two other major defects in economic planning. The first is that it stratifies and rigidizes the occupational structure of the nation. The very fact that it restricts the production of certain goods implies that it must prevent new producers from entering these fields. It creates a sort of vested right of those already engaged in a certain type of farming, or a certain occupation, to dominate these lines of production. Thus it is sure to stifle initiative, paralyze growth, and hold the country down to present—or even to lower—standards of living.

The other difficulty is that no economic planning can be effective unless it is on a world-wide basis. Raw materials are unevenly distributed among nations. Keen international competition in many lines of industry determines world prices. Hence the efforts of a single nation to plan its economic activities are affected not only by its dependence on foreign sources of raw materials but also by the internal reaction to world prices. Nothing short of hermetically sealed isolation can make a nation immune from the effects of world prices, and such isolation necessarily leads to lowered living standards.

Herein lies one of the greatest obstacles in the way of all economic planning. Of what use is it, for example, for the American government to hold down the size of the American cotton crop—a specific instance of economic planning—if, as a result of this policy, the cotton growers of Brazil and Egypt find it profitable to double their output? By paying subsidies to the American cotton farmers it is possible to create a temporary illusion of prosperity. But as a measure of permanent economic recovery this plan is doomed to fail because it is dependent on world forces which the American government cannot possibly control. In the process it transfers century-old markets for American cotton to foreign cotton growers, thus permanently impoverishing American cotton farmers and hence weakening the whole economic structure of the nation. It is paradoxical but true that economic nationalism cannot exist in a world made up of fifty different nations.

. . . .

If these various arguments against economic planning do not appear to be conclusive, it is only necessary to assume that planning can be carried out as its advocates believe possible, and then to ask the question: Suppose the planners were to make a major error in their plans? In other words, suppose that the planners are as likely to make mistakes as were the leading business men, bankers and economists at the beginning of the great depression, or as some of our political leaders during this same time and subsequently—would not the country face severe suffering and possibly even the gravest disaster if this plan were based on unforeseen errors of judgment or of fact?

. . . .

Impossible as is a government-directed planned economy, this does not mean that all planning about the economic development of the country is futile. But it is essential that planning begin from the ground up—that it be carried on intensively by localities and by states, and then perhaps by regions. Only when a great amount of research has been completed can any effective coordination be made and practical suggestions deduced for national guidance. Planning must begin in the community—not the nation.

Even then, any specific economic plan must be a mere chart of advisable cooperative action—not a mandatory measure imposed by force. Already the main outlines of procedure have been worked out by some of the municipal planning boards. These set desired goals and induce the local authorities to establish specific prohibitions, usually in the form of zoning laws. But such plans do not go beyond establishing broad policies—as that in certain sections no businesses may be conducted, or that there shall be a maximum height of buildings fronting a particular street, or that no building of more than a determined number of stories may be erected in given locations.

In such plans no provisions are made of a positive nature. There is, obviously, a great difference between a prohibition against erecting certain types of buildings or against using lands for particular purposes, and making it mandatory to erect specific buildings or to use certain lands. It is one thing for government to close lands to farmers or grazing. It is another for government to force settlers to cultivate other lands.

So also there is a difference between advice and compulsion—between, on the one hand, making plain to an occupational group the advisability to all concerned if it follows a particular policy for a given season, and, on the other hand, compelling by threat of punishment this same group to follow the same policy. The first way may not be quite as efficient, but at least it is true to the American tradition of individual initiative and freedom of action, whereas the second way is the way of paternalism—submission to dictation by a bureaucracy.

The defenders of some of the American experiments in applied planned economy have made much of the fact that in a number of instances the men who have submitted to control have done so of their own initiative—that they have, in fact, asked for control. If such requests were to come indisputably from an overwhelming majority of the group this argument would be impressive. But even though a small majority were to advocate control, and, in accordance with the theory of majority rule, were to seek to force control on the minority, the effect on this minority would be just the same as if the dictation were imposed without local ratification. As has been stressed in earlier chapters, governmental action can be just as hostile to the interests and rights of individuals when enforced by agents chosen by majorities as by agents of dictators.

It is not the sanction but the operation of economic planning that is the important thing—not the fact that farmers have accepted it when it is accompanied by generous government subsidies, but that economic planning, when put into effect, leads inevitably to control and compulsion. Necessarily it makes the economic structure rigid. And obviously it requires placing in the hands of the government enormous powers over individuals—powers to direct and to punish, to interfere and to hamper. How such powers can be exercised on a wide scale and over all economic activities without stifling initiative and degrading the individual into a mere tool of the state, is inconceivable. To make matters even worse, if there are mistakes in the plans—as there have been mistakes in all vast plans of all kinds since the beginning of organized society—planned economy is sure to end in unplanned disaster. It is the most dangerous of all the sirens of reformers.

HOW DEMOCRACIES DIE

XIII

DEMORALIZATION AND DEFAULT

CYNICS have often remarked that a people gets the kind of government it deserves. More accurate is it to say that if a people does not care what kind of government it has, it will be given the kind of government that its politicians want. Citizens exercise a marked influence over public affairs only so long as they are actively interested in public questions and in principles and practices of government. When their interest wanes their influence ceases.

This is particularly true in popular government, as John Stuart Mill brought out nearly three-quarters of a century ago. "A people," he said in the very beginning of his famous essay on Representative Government, "may prefer a free government; but if, from indolence, or carelessness, or cowardice, or want of public spirit, they are unequal to the exertions necessary for preserving it; if they will not fight for it when it is directly attacked; if they can be deluded by the artifices used to cheat them out of it; if, by momentary discouragement, or temporary panic, or a fit of enthusiasm for an individual, they can be induced to lay their liberties at the feet even of a great man, or trust him with powers which

201

enable him to subvert their institutions—in all these cases they are more or less unfit for liberty; and though it may be for their good to have had it even for a short time, they are unlikely long to enjoy it."

Mill's diagnosis may not be the last word on how democracies die. But it is a penetrating—and painfully true—observation by a great student of politics and history. Certain it is that liberty—or a free government—or what we are now accustomed to call "democracy"—is not imperishable, and that it is unlikely to last long when the people lose interest in it. It is also clear that popular government does not fit the needs and abilities of all peoples. The Latin American republics are notable examples of this truth. Free government can only function effectively when its growth has been slow and its roots have gone deep into traditions and customs. It cannot be handed to a people on a platter—or to use the metaphor of the late Dean C. Worcester in criticizing the American policy of forcing free government on the Filipinos, "the practical way is to let the apple hang high and make them climb for it, instead of telling them to hold their hats and shake the tree."

Forms of democracy are empty unless the people have the habit of self-government and will infuse the spirit of free men into the legal frame of a free government. As Aristotle pointed out, good laws or a good constitution do not, by themselves, make good government. Besides having good laws a people must be ready to obey the laws and to accept the authority of the constitution, and the laws and constitution must be fairly enforced. This implies self-restraint and cooperation, together with a sense of responsibility to the community. Furthermore it assumes a spirit of "obedience to the unenforceable"—of a willingness to abide by the unwritten rules of the game.

Obvious as is the intrinsic relation between the character and traditions of a people and its form of government, and extensive as has been the study of different kinds of government since the days of Plato, no one, including that ingenious philosopher, has determined whether there is any consistent pathology of governments, and whether, when changes in governmental forms occur, these follow a fixed pattern. Plato postulated a cycle of changes: aristocracy (or government for all by the best) giving way to oligarchy (or government by a small class of rich people for that class) followed by democracy (or government by the many) giving way to tyranny (or dictatorship by a demagogue) followed by a reversion to a form of aristocracy. While some of the sequences of change which he discussed are plausible enough, it is obvious that he was toying with theories rather than considering political practices.

Even if any such cycle had recurred with regularity prior to Plato's own day, the democratic city states which existed for brief periods in Greece, like the various Republics, including that of early Rome, which were known prior to 1789, show no clear precedents that serve to throw much light on the pathology of modern democracies. Historians and professors of political economy gave little thought to this subject before the end of the World War. In fact, so confident had the Western world been, down to 1914, that democracy was the final and perfect flowering of governmental forms that no one considered the possibility, let alone the possible causes, of its death. The keenest student of comparative democracies, Lord Bryce, described the forms and functions, rather than the growth and decline, of modern democracies. Since he published his two volumes on this subject in 1921, a wave of anti-democracy has swept over the world, and one so-called democratic or republican government after another has been wiped out.

Why this anti-democratic movement has been so successful is a problem still to be solved. At best only a few brief suggestions may, as yet, be tentatively put forward. Most of these center about the demoralization of the democratic principle and the growing contempt of the people for professional politicians. The same reasons have not operated with equal force in all countries. It is noticeable that the swing away from popular or parliamentary government has been most extreme in those countries in which the traditions of self-government were weakest. But the symptoms are in evidence even in countries which still retain the form as well as the substance of popular government. The sickness which has afflicted democracies is contagious. No one yet knows if it is fatal.

The process by which democracy has been discredited seems to have been about as follows:

(1) The lowering of the calibre of legislative assemblies due to the growing indifference of the people about public affairs, and to the reluctance of men of ability, intelligence and character to run for elective office.

(2) The increasing contempt of the people for all politicians due to their selfishness and lack of integrity and courage, and for all bureaucrats due to their capacity for inaction.

(3) Impatience with the long-windedness of most parliamentarians, and boredom with their public addresses.

(4) The feeling that legislative bodies do not and cannot achieve anything—that all they do is talk, and never act.

(5) The war-time lesson that in a crisis a strong executive is essential.

(6) The corollary of this—that in a great economic crisis it is necessary to empower the government to take any steps that may be needed to save the nation.

(7) The increasing sense of bafflement of the people as the problems of economic recovery prove as hard to solve as the problems of the war.

(8) The resulting sense of helplessness which has

made men anxious to find a leader who will solve their problems for them and save them from disaster.

(9) The readiness of people to seek a scapegoat, which leads them naturally to blame the existing economic and political "system" for their troubles, and so to hope that changes may bring about better times.

(10) The influence of the radical doctrine that only new remedies can solve the new problems, and that unless something drastic is done we shall all be pulled under by the "system."

Less tangible, but perhaps even more important, is the glamor that attaches to strong men—a glamor which is all the greater in countries where rank and pomp have long been absent. The great political heroes of the world —the Alexanders, the Cæsars, the Napoleons, the Mussolinis—not only have been the great doers of the world, but have captivated men's imagination and loyalty. To persons bowed down by the drab struggle to survive there is something inspiring, enlarging, even ennobling, in the thought of an Augustus, conquering the world and bringing order out of chaos. This is why the officeholder so often overshadows the office—and why there is a natural inclination to prefer a single glamorous figure, like a President, to the uninspiring mediocrity of a legislative group. If modern democracies were not so inseparably tied up with parliaments and congresses it might be harder to discredit them. Who can be thrilled by a dull page in the Congressional Record? How few, *per contra*, fail to respond to a highly dramatic Fuehrer or Duce?

That the above reasons are the only ones why democracies have been discredited, or that the phenomena which they list lead inevitably to the destruction of democracy, is not to be believed. But, reinforced by other trends, they indicate symptoms that may not be lightly ignored.

Take, for example, what has happened in the United States. No one questions the loss of faith in politicians which has become more widespread every decade. Nor is there doubt that the average American no longer knows or understands much about the fundamentals of the American system. He has, it is true, a blind faith in the perfection of the American form of government, but this faith is not reasoned and is vague rather than specific. Certainly it is not strong enough to induce him to take a direct interest in public affairs. He is, in fact, so far removed from active participation in politics that he has even lost the tradition of local self-government. If, as is now the case with at least a third of our people, he is descended from the races of Central, Southern or Eastern Europe he lacks the heritage and background of popular government which the colonists and immigrants from Northern Europe had. If he does not share the Eastern Europeans' hatred of the agents of government his attitude toward them is one of dislike based on his experience with policemen and tax collectors who have seemed unfair, unreasonable, and inefficient.

As if this were not enough the American people have been subjected since the great depression to a subtle propaganda discrediting those qualities of personal initiative and self-reliance on which free government is dependent, and even ridiculing the sacrifices of the pioneers and early settlers who made self-government part of the nation's heritage. Children of the airplane and motor age have little understanding of the incredible hardships that the pioneers endured in building up America. They have no appreciation of the permanent value of those qualities of character which were necessary if a pioneer people were to survive. Americans today, instead of depending on themselves, expect to be helped. Instead of doing their part in the community they expect the community to support them. Instead of regarding government as an umpire, to be turned to only when the rules of the game are in dispute, they have come to look on government as the proper purveyor of all that they want. They welcome—they even demand—paternalism, and are frankly indifferent to "old fogey" notions about personal liberty, popular government and democracy.

That this has made fruitful soil for demagogues is obvious. And it is not surprising, under the circumstances, to see that Plato's description of the ways of the demagogue has a strangely modern sound. "At first," he wrote in Book VIII of the "Republic," "in the early days of his power, he is full of smiles, and he salutes every one whom he meets; he to be called a dictator, who is making promises in public and also in private! Liberating debtors, and distributing land to the people and his followers, and wanting to be so kind and good to every one!" Later—like Mussolini or Hitler—he asks for a bodyguard—and does not hesitate to "purge" the country of his enemies. He pursues the money-changers —Plato made no references to Jews—and confiscates the property of the wealthy, and in all of this he has the support of the people who look upon him as their champion.

Who can doubt that the trust placed in such a man is due to the combination of his own lure and of the people's hopelessness and indifference? The people turn to a glamorous leader because he poses as their friend, but they do so all the more readily because they are not interested in abstract political doctrines or in questions of governmental forms.

This indifference is the most dangerous of all the factors of disintegration in democracies today. It is a revival of a frame of mind that persisted throughout Europe for a thousand years, and which is symptomatic of a sick society. When men no longer care, they are on the verge of demoralization. Workers who are uninterested in their work produce shoddy goods. Business men who are indifferent to their business face failure. Professional men who lack zest for their professions will never make good. When a people is indifferent to its government it cannot expect that government long to endure.

Popular government is, as Mill indicated, particularly susceptible to popular indifference. Its dependence on the interest and support of the people for its effective functioning means that when this interest is slight, and support of the government is grudging, democracy loses its vitality. When this happens democracy falls a ready prey to plutocracy or to any man or group eager to remake the form of government.

The money power has ever been as ready to corrupt democracy as to influence other forms of government. It does this all the more easily when the forces of democracy have been weakened through a loss of interest in political principles. So also, the wider the gap between the people and the actual administrative and legislative officers, the easier it is for politicians to effect important structural changes in the government—and to do so almost unnoticed. When the agents of government are no longer close to the people, the people lose interest in their government. If changes are proposed the people pay little heed because they realize that it is futile to protest. When, in contrast, a truly popular government is well-established and the people feel in touch with their political leaders, opposition to fundamental changes can readily make itself felt. But the effectiveness of opposition depends on a continuing popular interest in public affairs—the kind of interest which, at least down to the beginning of the twentieth century, was widespread in America. Men and women—and even boys—in those days were keen about politics—and the mass judgment seemed almost instinctively right.

In this connection I often think of a remark Colonel Theodore Roosevelt made to a group of young cousins during the 1912 "Bull Moose" campaign. The conversation had turned to the ability of a large body of voters to pass intelligently on a question of national policy. One of the most striking lessons of his political experience, the former President said, was how invariably the American people, once they had all the facts in a case put before them, made a right decision. It was only when part of the facts were withheld, or when they were hurried into a choice without time for full consideration, that they decided wrongly. Implicit in this observation based on thirty years of active participation in politics was the assumption that the people took a continuing interest in public affairs.

Since the World War indifference has become widespread in America. The fatuous phrase, "O.K., Chief!" contains almost as much power of destruction as a bomb. If it merely connoted blind obedience, it would be bad enough. But it implies hearty satisfaction at being relieved from having to consider public questions. It is a form of "passing the buck"—and passing it with all the more gusto in that those who use the phrase expect the government to whom the buck is passed to relieve them of all further need even to consider—let alone to solve—the problems of the day.

In yielding all initiative to the government the individual is taking a course of easy selfishness, indifferent to all but his desire to be relieved of the difficulty of thought. Why, he asks, should he bother his head about checks and balances, about federalism and states' rights, about civil liberties? Let lawyers and professors quarrel about these outmoded terms. It is up to government to help him, and if it can't do it under the present form, then change it.

What he fails to see is that if he accepts the new gospel that democracy and the Constitution are outmoded shibboleths and that the country should have, instead, the kind of government that will assure him what he wants, the politicians in power will change the government to suit, not his, but their needs. In proportion to his indifference to them they will disregard and scorn him.

In the final analysis the fate of democracy in America will be determined by the willingness of the American people to make the necessary sacrifices to preserve the American system. If they do not care enough about it, the system will surely be discarded. Democracy is particularly vulnerable in the face of any determined, well-organized group. It is necessarily loosely organized and clumsy, whereas an autocratic government is closely knit and efficient. At best it is government by compromise, whereas autocracy is government by force. Democracy assumes opposition and expects rotation in office. Autocracy denies the right to oppose and rejects with the death sentence the claim of others to displace it from office. Democracy is based on discussion and on a weighing of the conflicting claims of minority groups. Autocracy stifles discussion and recognizes only one minority —the minority in power. In the modern world autocracy is once more ascendent—and autocracy asks nothing better of the surviving democracies than that their people become indifferent to their governments and lose faith in democracy as a way of life.

XIV

DICTATORSHIP AND DESIGN

THE TRADITIONAL way in which forms of government have been changed is by revolution. How, then, has revolution been conceived and executed?

Obviously not by the masses, however active may have been the subsequent participation of the people in an organized revolt. True, popular discontent with the existing order has usually been indispensable to the successful execution of any revolution. But the inspiration and the impetus has come from a mere handful of planners, and sometimes from a single dominant and domineering personality backed by a band of devoted and fearless followers. Fighting has not necessarily preceded a successful coup d'état. Mussolini and Hitler came to power with little direct bloodshed. In Russia the Kerensky government was overthrown by a carefully planned coup carried out by a few soldiers and technicians through the simultaneous seizure of important government buildings and of the transportation, light and water systems of Petrograd.

But revolutionary changes have been brought about by less dramatic and noticeable means than a coup d'état. Aristotle, whose chapter on revolution in his "Politics"

214

still stands out as one of the most enlightening discussions on this subject, pointed out that revolutions often are effected almost unperceived. Let him explain in his own words: "Sometimes the citizens are deceived into a change of government, and afterwards they are held in subjection against their will," he says. And again, "The citizens begin by giving up some part of the constitution, and so with greater ease the government changes something else which is a little more important, until it has undermined the whole fabric of the state."

And again: "Revolutions in democracies are generally caused by the intemperance of demagogues, who either in their private capacity lay information against rich men until they compel them to combine (for common danger unites even the bitterest enemies), or coming forward in public they stir up the people against them. . . . Sometimes the demagogues, in order to curry favor with the people, wrong the notables . . . either they make a division of their property, or diminish their incomes by the imposition of public services, and sometimes they bring accusations against the rich that they may have their wealth to confiscate."

"Governments also change into oligarchy or into democracy or into a constitutional government," Aristotle explains, "because the magistrates, or some other section of the state, increase in power or renown. . . . And generally, it should be remembered that those who have secured power to the state, whether private citizens, or magistrates, or tribes, or any other part or section of the state, are apt to cause revolutions. For either envy of their greatness draws others into rebellion, or they themselves, in their pride of superiority, are unwilling to remain on a level with others." And again, "History shows that almost all tyrants have been demagogues who gained the favor of people by their accusation of the notables."

Giving advice on how revolutions can be avoided, Aristotle warned that men should guard against the beginnings of change, and added: "In all well-attempered governments there is nothing which should be more jealously maintained than the spirit of obedience to law, more especially in small matters; for transgression creeps in unperceived and at last ruins the state, just as the constant recurrence of small expenses in time eats up a fortune. The change does not take place all at once, and therefore is not observed."

Translated into modern terms these observations of Aristotle teach that a carefully worked out plan of a small and determined group can bring about fundamental changes in the form of the state before the people are aware of what has happened. Even when, as in the case of Hitler, power was seized through orderly and apparently constitutional procedure, the real revolution —the scrapping of the Weimar constitution and the creation of the new nazi state—was effected with surprising speed before the German people had any idea of what was happening. Even those who had neither hope nor faith in Hitler were little alarmed by changes the effects of which they could not foresee, and which they were powerless to prevent. They did not realize that the dreams of German republicans, socialists and communists had gone up in the smoke of the Reichstag fire out of which arose the phœnix of the nazi state-all-powerful.

Those revolutionaries who have forcibly seized the power of a state are the more obvious—and, at least in so far as the popular governments that still survive today are concerned, the less dangerous—enemies. Theirs is the mode of most Latin-American dictators. Some, like Mussolini and Hitler, besides being brave and skilful agitators, owed their initial success in large part to their capacity as orators and actors. Their appeal was intensely dramatic and personal, and was so couched that they could pose as saviors of the nation. But they fought for power openly and vigorously, and made no secret before they were in office of what they would do when they finally triumphed. To be sure, both men were astute opportunists—as is every great political leader —but they made little effort to deceive the people, and did not try to hide their intentions under a false front.

No one expects a Mussolini or a Hitler—or even a Huey Long—to seize power by force in the United States or in one of the British dominions. Here the danger is from a more subtle type—from a disciple of Augustus rather than of Julius Cæsar—from a man who, while paying lip-service to existing forms, seeks to change their basic substance unperceived, rather than from one who openly seeks to scrap constitutional government.

That such a man might perform as great a service to the United States as Augustus did to the Empire is conceivable—if a man as wise, temperate and far-seeing as Augustus could be found. In the Rome of his day men of all classes turned to Augustus and begged him to save them and to solve their problems. Eagerly they granted him all the powers that he asked for. They were not interested in liberty, but in security. He gave them, in addition, prosperity, and they worshipped him as a god. What they wanted was peace and public order—stability rather than self-government. He was wise enough to provide this and to build an administrative machine that was efficient and free from corruption. His constant preoccupation was to pay the utmost respect to old-established Roman institutions and to revive and revere Roman traditions. Thus he divested himself of the appearance of a dictator imposing a new deal on Rome. At the same time he made sure that full and final power was concentrated in his own hands, even though he delegated much of this to other officials and periodically went through the forms of seeking public ratification of his acts. So long as he had the substance of power he gladly left to others its shadow.

The tolerance, fairness and efficiency of the new government of Augustus comforted those who deplored the passing of the republic and who sensed the dangers inherent in a permanent dictatorship. It was not until his successors proved the lesson which mankind seems never willing to learn—that there is no way of insuring the succession of a benevolent dictator by another equally benevolent dictator—that the Roman people began to realize that the shell of the old Roman state to which Augustus had given a fresh luster housed an entirely new type of government. The new Rome had as little in common with the Rome of the pre-Julian period as Stalin's Russia had with the Russia of the Czars. But so repeatedly had Augustus insisted that he was merely restoring and rejuvenating the old republic, and that his innovations were based on old traditions, that people failed to grasp that during his long public service he substituted a bureaucracy dominated by a personal autocrat for the old Roman republic to which he paid so much tribute.

Apart from the skill with which Augustus reorganized the state, he stands out supreme because of his moderation, his unselfishness, and his high sense of responsibility for the welfare of his people. Probably few of his successors, with the possible exception of the late Austrian Emperor Franz Josef, had Augustus's sense of an Emperor's duty to serve. But Franz Josef ruled over only a small remnant of the Roman empire, and was a man with a meticulous mind and no vision.

The Augustan tactics may well be attempted by an

individual or group seeking to transform the American form of representative government into a collectivist state. The only real stumbling block is the Supreme Court. A President with a large subservient majority in Congress can impose such laws on the country as he deems necessary. If the laws are sufficiently long and involved in their wording to confuse even intelligent critics and commentators, it is a simple matter for the Administration in power to lull all suspicion and stifle opposition by insisting in interviews and in radio addresses that the new laws are entirely in accordance with American traditions. Only after the new laws have been challenged in the courts and, on appeal, brought before the Supreme Court, can they be effectively checked.

This is why so many radical reformers have so persistently attacked the Supreme Court and have urged that it be brought under the control of the executive branch of the government. They know that so long as the Supreme Court is filled by honorable and fearless men, and—fully as important—so long as its prestige among the people remains unimpaired, it can hold the American form of government to its intended pattern, and, in particular, it can halt those collectivist laws which by their very nature would tend subtly but surely to change the fundamental structure of the government.

European socialists have pointed out how the collectivist objective may be achieved by this sort of indirection in countries where the parliamentary or congressional form of government is still valued. They do not advocate resort to the so-called "evolutionary" tactics, through which a socialist party would simply seek to obtain a majority in Congress, and also elect its own President and other officials. Nor do they propose the communist system of "boring from within," by which a small group might seek to obtain power within existing frameworks. Rather would the method be based largely on deliberate deception through constant reiteration of devotion to the old forms of government at the same time that these forms are subtly undermined.

The English radical, C. D. H. Cole, in his "What Marx Really Meant," has indicated in general lines how such a transformation of a parliamentary state into a socialist state might be attempted. The objective of those in charge of establishing a socialist government is, he points out, to destroy "as soon as it can the very foundations on which the opportunities for capitalist profit-making rest." Inasmuch as capitalist prosperity is largely a matter of capitalist confidence—"confidence, that is, in the prospect of sustained profit-making" is his definition—it follows that this confidence must be undermined.

But a socialist government must keep capitalist institutions at work until it is prepared to take them over. As this is hard without winning the confidence of the capitalists, the system must be kept running without that confidence—"that is to say," Cole candidly explains, "by making the conditions even more unfavorable to the capitalist who closes his business down, or contracts its operation owing to his loss of confidence, than to the capitalist who maintains employment and output despite his dislike and distrust of the socialist government. This can be secured only if the government is prepared to take over, confiscate and operate any useful businesses which their owners elect to close or to contract, and if, further, a strong control is promptly established over all businesses which are to be left in private hands during the earlier stages of transition to socialism."

Cole, like Marx, accepts the idea that any effective transformation of this sort can only be made through the dictatorship of a small class, even though the dictators claim to work in the name of the proletariat. Neither believes that any such change can be brought about openly by mass action. Both reject the idea of a movement in the name of the people as a whole, as this precludes the concept of classes, and class warfare is deemed indispensable to the success of communism. At the same time, both recognize the necessity of crushing all opposition, and of "purging" all those elements that disagree with or might endanger the new rulers. No doubt both would consider the "blood purges" of Stalin and Hitler as unavoidable under the circumstances, and therefore justifiable.

It is important, in considering this subject, not to be

misled by the quarrels between the apostles of various collectivist creeds as to differences between the objectives of radical socialism or communism on the one hand, and national socialism or fascism on the other. The essential point, at least in so far as the surviving democratic countries are concerned, is that all the totalitarian systems propose to place in the hands of the state vast powers to control the economic activities of the people as a whole. They envisage a state which, if it does not actually own all the machinery of production—i.e., all business, transportation and agriculture—at least dominates them so completely that individuals have no alternative but to work as the state dictates.

It is this creation of vast new instruments of public power in the hands of a self-styled "people's government" which is likely, sooner or later, to provide those very shackles of the liberties of the people which President Roosevelt recently deplored. Whether such powers are granted in the name of socialism or popular government matters little. What counts in the United States is that these powers can be used by unscrupulous leaders for the overthrow of the existing order, once the Supreme Court of the United States has been taken over or curbed, or has been denied the right to pass on the constitutionality of acts of Congress and the President.

Two other methods exist by which democratic governments can be subtly transformed into autocracies. One is by resort to inflation and the other is by resort to war.

The former paves the way for a "strong" government because it wipes out those forces of stability personified in the "middle classes"—the men and women with small incomes and small investments and savings who in every age have constituted the "backbone of the nation." These are the people who suffer first and most severely when a country resorts to inflation, for, even though their small debts may be wiped out, their savings and their earning capacity are also destroyed and, in consequence, their living standards are lowered. In the economic chaos that follows inflation they find it virtually impossible to survive, and hence cease to have any direct interest in the perpetuation or revival of the old system. In their desperation they welcome any leader who promises to save them and to restore economic order, and gladly see him clothed with dictatorial powers.

There is no doubt, for example, that the inflation in Germany, more even than defeat in the World War, paved the way for Hitler's rise to power. Had not the German middle classes been ruined they might well have been able to bolster up the nascent republic or to have effected the restoration of a constitutional monarchy. Certainly they would never have given whole-hearted approval to extensive experiments in a form of state capitalism that promises to enslave small business men and farmers and to impoverish the nation as a whole.

There is, as yet, no recorded instance of a government

deliberately adopting a policy of inflation for ulterior political purposes. But, because inflation ruins the middle classes and brings about economic chaos, it can be a useful technique in achieving revolution. By increasing discontent it makes it easier to discredit the old order, and to blame all the momentary ills on the "system" rather than on the inflation. The possibility of its use should not be disregarded in considering the dangers that threaten democracy.

The other expedient—resort to war—is one of the age-old devices of political leaders who wish to distract attention from troubles at home. Like inflation, it has not yet been used deliberately to change the form of government. But, at least in the United States, it affords an accepted—if not a constitutional—method of establishing a dictatorship. The old Roman custom—before the days of the Empire—was to grant dictatorial powers for a period of six months. The American practice is to grant such powers "for the duration of the emergency." Precedents established during the Civil War and the World War, together with laws recently enacted or proposed, give the President virtually supreme control over everything and everybody in the United States the moment a state of war exists. While this presupposes a formal declaration of war by Congress, recent worldwide experience has shown that bloody wars can be fought between nations still formally at peace. An unscrupulous President, thwarted in his attempts to obtain full powers in peacetime, might well be tempted to go to war for the sole purpose of being able, in consequence, to make himself omnipotent.

It is the strong men—the unscrupulous men—who, in the final analysis, are the active enemies of democracy. Whether or not they are mere egotists, or, like Julius and Augustus Cæsar and Napoleon, they have a passion for order and hence find the delays and inefficiencies of popular government intolerable, is only incidental. They have the will—and the ability—to override the masses— which is probably why democracy is instinctively distrustful of strong men. In America, the entire political system is built up with a view to making it impossible for strong men to break the bonds set by the Constitution and the laws.

Because of this latent hostility, fascists and communists alike are impatient with democracy. They know that fascism—and even communism, as Marx was frank to admit—can only be imposed by a strong man, or a group of strong men, seizing power in one or another manner and proceeding by the unscrupulous use of violence, as well as of cunning, to overthrow the existing order and to establish in its stead the kind of government that the strong men wish to impose. Hence fascists and communists side with the strong men against democracy, and pour ridicule on the incompetence and the stupidity of the masses. This is Europe's challenge to America today, and not even America's geographical isolation

226

makes the nation immune to the contagion of Europe's "strong man" doctrine.

History shows, in fact, that there is a close interrelation between political trends on both sides of the Atlantic. Sometimes, as in the practice of political liberalism, America has been ahead of most of Europe, and sometimes, as in the development of governmental measures of social welfare, it has been behind. But the great movements of reform and reaction have, in general, coincided. The American and French revolutions were only a few years apart. Each was followed by a wave of reaction which, in the case of Europe, swept over the continent. On both sides of the Atlantic there were popular uprisings in the '30s and '40s of the last century, followed by a trend toward conservatism in the '50s and '60s. The last quarter of the nineteenth century was marked by a combination of political and economic conservatism, with a more liberal swing in the years just before the war.

Since 1920, the trend everywhere has been toward extreme reaction, whether in the form of authoritarianism, national conservatism or modified state socialism. The parliamentary system has been discredited or discarded in most of Europe. Dictatorships have risen in the place of democracies or republics. In the United States, after a dozen years of reactionary republicanism based on the nineteenth-century doctrine of non-interference by government, the country has taken a plunge into executive nationalism on a scale never before witnessed in peacetime. The fact that this has been done under a liberal and radical terminology should not obscure the nature of the changes that have been initiated. Whether they be good or bad is not the point in question. The important thing to bear in mind is that the changes in America in many ways parallel those in Europe, and that many of them are due to the contagion of reactionary ideas.

Nor is this all. The Spanish revolution of 1936-8 has shown that political doctrines are still the subject of armed strife in our own age. While it is probably an exaggeration to conclude that German and Italian help was given in Spain solely in order to establish a new fascist state, there can be no doubt that the Germans and Italians would regard an addition to the company of fascist states as beneficial to the prestige of the fascist doctrine. Certainly Russian aid in Spain was given for the purpose of preventing a fascist victory. It goes without saying that, if the principle of non-official intervention by fascist states in support of all new fascist governments becomes well established, there may be political consequences which could seriously embarrass not only all of non-fascist Europe but also Latin America and the United States. The same is true of communist intervention and support.

Suppose, for example, that fascism or communism were to spread in Latin America, and that German or Italian airplanes and volunteers were to take active part in support of Latin-American fascists, or Russian and

Mexican provocateurs in support of communism. Could the United States sit by with folded hands? Fascism, like communism, is opposed to everything that the American people have believed in and fought for. It represents in modern form the same kind of reaction against which the Monroe Doctrine was originally proclaimed. So long as fascism or communism is adopted by foreign nations through the process of self-determination, America cannot interfere. But when they are propagated by fire and sword in neighbor nations, and by propagandists in this country, they cease to be doctrinaire questions for political theorists and become explosive factors in practical politics.

Fascism, like communism, has acquired something of the moral fervor of a crusade. Men seem more ready to die to promote or prevent fascism or communism than to defend democracy. Both are paternalistic in philosophy, and reject the whole concept of popular government. They are openly hostile to democracy and liberalism. To them Lincoln's ideal of a government of the people, for the people and by the people, is mere foolishness. Both have their eager apostles preaching, and sometimes subtly scheming, to overthrow popular government wherever it has survived. Is their challenge to be received without protest? Is democracy to fold its hands in impotence and face death without a struggle?

RESURGENT FEDERALISM

XV

BACK TO SELF-GOVERNMENT

EXECUTIVE nationalism—a strongly centralized, all-powerful government in Washington—is destructive of popular government. It is reaction, not progress—the way of empire, not of democracy.

What, then, should be the new objective, and how may it be attained?

In politics as in economics the goal is decentralization. The late Ogden L. Mills well phrased it when he said that "nothing should be transferred to the larger unit which can adequately be performed by the smaller."

What would this mean in practice?

To begin with, it calls for the strengthening of the state governments by improving their personnel and, in most cases, by modernizing their constitutions. There is no reason why, in the process, each state should not alter its social and governmental structure as its citizens desire—and as the Constitution of the United States permits. There are potential limitations on this process due to the fact that the Federal Constitution expressly provides that the Federal government shall "guarantee to each state a republican form of government." But the courts have declined to define just what such a republican form of government is, and in practice the state governments have varied from types of oligarchy—as in the South—to state socialism—and even, during the heyday of Huey Long—to a one-man dictatorship on the nazi model.

Variety of state governmental forms should be deliberately encouraged, for it is through practical political experimentation by the states that the most helpful contributions can be made to the science of self-government. Much is to be learned from the mistakes, as well as from the successes, of these experiments. North Dakota's venture in state capitalism, for example, has shown the weakness of this as a form of government. Wisconsin's land zoning and state aid to agriculture have opened new fields of usefulness in sound government planning and administration. Oregon and Washington have experimented with the initiative, the referendum and the recall sufficiently to convince most students that, however compelling the logic of these extensions of applied democracy may be, they hold little hope of correcting the abuses in the existing system against which they were originally aimed.

If I may drop for a moment the realism which has characterized the analyses in this book and indulge in speculative thinking, it is possible to envisage the Federal Union in the not-too-distant future embracing not only the traditional forms of state governments, but others representing drastic politico-economic innovations. Some of the states might attempt to adapt the commission form of government that has proved successful in various cities. A few might copy the governments of some of the British Dominions. Others might go even further than have North Dakota and Minnesota in establishing state control of business and farming—always provided that in these changes they do not infringe the basic rights of minorities and do not curtail fundamental civil liberties. A wide latitude in forms of state government is altogether in keeping with sound principles of free self-government. The British Commonwealth of Nations is a notable example of a union of autonomous states with a variety of governmental forms.

As already indicated in earlier chapters, one of the advantages of the American federal system is that state borders limit the harm resulting from mistakes made by particular state governments. Only the people of the erring state are the victims of their politicians' errors. The people in other states escape them.

Huey Long's dictatorship in Louisiana is a case in point. His government differed only in name from that of a Mussolini or a Hitler. He dominated Louisiana as a personal dictator, backed by an armed bodyguard, and even sat on the floor of the legislature with machine gunners in the aisles as he dictated the passage of the laws he wanted. There is little doubt that his success in Louisiana led him to look forward to an extension of his empire.

There is equally little doubt that Huey's dictatorship was restricted to Louisiana by state lines. He could control Louisiana, but he could not as directly or as completely control Mississippi or Arkansas—unless he were to attempt a coup d'état such as Hitler put over in Austria, followed by an armed invasion of the neighbor state. Such armed invasion would have imposed on the Federal government the duty of using the United States Army to protect the invaded state.

But the new federalism calls for more than the development and strengthening of the states as political entities—for more than greatly increased state powers of control and regulation of economic activities. Two other developments are essential—one downward, through the extension of the principle of home rule to all large cities; and the other outward, through the more frequent use of state compacts to deal with regional problems.

The first of these developments is in no sense an innovation. It has been urged for years by students of municipal government and by persons who have had experience in city politics. The purpose is obvious—to enable the cities to run their own affairs without being dependent on state legislatures which are often hostile to urban interests. Why, for example, should Albany have control over New York City, or Springfield, Illinois, over Chicago? The mere statement of the question suggests the answer.

The case for regionalism is less familiar, although in

recent years state compacts have been occasionally formed. Most of the theoretical discussion of regionalism has centered about abolishing state lines and creating in place of the states a number of larger territorial units or commonwealths, so formed as to unite regions bound together by geographical and occupational ties. New England, for example, would be one such commonwealth; Greater New York City would be another; Pennsylvania, Maryland, Delaware and New Jersey might form a third, etc.

The arguments in behalf of regional commonwealths are usually of two sorts. The first, concerned with politics, is that the new units would make it easier for Washington to administer the affairs of the nation by decentralizing the national government into regional governments. The second, concerned with economics, is that the new regions would be geographically and economically unitary, based on common economic interests, and that the control of economic conditions by the commonwealth governments would be simpler and more effective than the present divided control by the states and the Federal government.

Against this sort of regionalism several forceful arguments can be made. The first and most obvious is of a constitutional nature. Such commonwealths could not be formed without rewriting the Federal Constitution. This, in itself, virtually excludes regional commonwealths as actual possibilities. Next in importance are the imponderables of tradition and of local loyalties. These are, in many cases, deeply rooted. Despite the frequent movement of Americans from one state to another, and despite the comparatively recent settlement of many of the western states, strong attachments to the states exist, and there is little reason to believe that a majority of the people would willingly give up their state loyalty for a larger regional allegiance.

This is as true in regions which, like the "Solid South," are united by tradition and history, as in the Middle or Far West. The Virginians have so long been convinced of their superiority over the North Carolinians that they look upon the latter almost as "furriners." The Nebraskans are certain that they are superior to the more earthbound citizens of Iowa. To go from Cincinnati, Ohio, to Louisville, Kentucky—scarcely 100 miles away—is to pass into an entirely different civilization with different ideals, traditions and aspirations.

These differences cannot—nor should—be ironed out. There is little to be gained by arbitrary conformity. Most standardization—except of bare utilities—is drab and degrading. The valuable contributions to civilization have come from disparity, not from levelling uniformity. The various states, both new and old, already have distinct individuality. New York is not New Jersey. Arizona and Oregon belong to different worlds. Mississippi differs from Vermont in appearance, in history and in economic, political and social ambitions.

Even if the constitutional, social and cultural objections to regional commonwealths were immaterial and irrelevant, there is no reason to believe that the creation of such commonwealths either would insure better government than is furnished by the states, or would actually facilitate the kind of decentralization which many persons desire. Unless there were to be an entirely new method of selecting officers for the commonwealths the chances are that the same kind of men would run for governor and for the commonwealth legislatures as now run for state offices. Once in power they would be as jealous of the Federal government as are the states, and the Federal bureaucracy, in turn, would be as unwilling to decentralize power into the hands of regional commonwealths as it has been eager to enlarge its powers at the expense of the states. The only practical result would be the substitution of larger, even more clumsy units of government for the present states.

Even if the regional governments were to be mere administrative subdivisions of a central government with officers appointed by that government, it is very doubtful if the politicians in Washington would surrender any part of their power to the regions, however compelling might be the administrative need of decentralization. The temptation to hold and control the vast patronage that would thus be within their grasp would be irresistible.

The impracticability of creating new commonwealths

does not mean, however, that regional cooperation is ruled out in the United States. Quite the contrary. Regional cooperation has its place within the Federal system. While many problems are essentially national, there are many others which concern only two or three or a small group of states. Such, for instance, are the disposal of sewage in and about Greater New York, and the administration of state park lands adjoining in New Jersey and New York. There is no reason why these should be settled by Federal intervention. They are proper matters to be handled directly by the states concerned.

Regional cooperation, as the term itself suggests, is based on the interests of particular regions—regions which, as a rule, are unified by geographical or economic ties—or both. There is no reason, for example, why such projects as the T.V.A. or the Colorado River development should be paid for by the people of the nation as a whole and administered by the Federal government. They are of strictly regional concern. The principal beneficiaries of the T.V.A. are the people in the states immediately adjoining the experiment. The people of California and Arizona, more even than those of Nevada, in which Boulder City is situated, are the chief beneficiaries of the Colorado River project. In like manner the proposed compact between the New England States for the control of the waters of the Connecticut River basin is a New England project. It should be handled by New Englanders for New England. There is no possible justification for the interference of the Federal government to prevent such an agreement.

Cooperation between the states is in keeping with American traditions. Pioneering was in no sense anti-cooperative. It was not individualism, rank and undefiled, even though it put a premium on individual initiative. Each pioneer family sought its own land and worked it alone, but, as I have already explained in Chapter VII, when there was a community problem to be solved, the neighbors joined in. If a road was to be built—or, in the dry country, an irrigation ditch to be dug to serve a number of neighbors—they got together and arranged to apportion the work. If problems affecting larger groups were at issue, they met for the express purpose of working out a solution in the joint interest. They did not invoke the aid of Washington, or even of the state capital.

What the pioneer communities did the states can do, even though the fact that, under the Constitution, no state compacts can be made without Congressional sanction, has served to discourage this method of procedure. The practical political obstacles in the way of negotiating state compacts do not mean that such a policy cannot be developed successfully. In numerous instances recently it has been resorted to, and the practice is certain to become more common as its advantages are more appreciated. To date it has suffered more from disuse than from any inherent defect in the system itself.

Remains, of course, the problem of the so-called "no-man's" land, where neither the Federal nor state governments have as yet managed to establish effective control. Due to ambiguities in the Federal Constitution, and to conflicting decisions of the courts, there are cases in which it is doubtful whether either the Federal or a state government has jurisdiction. The advocates of centralization demand that whenever neither Federal nor state governments can deal with problems, the Federal government should be empowered to act. The advocates of decentralization reply that the states should be enabled to exercise the necessary control—that they are the logical bodies to regulate economic problems.

The point at issue is no merely doctrinaire problem of states' rights, no abstract theory of sovereignty. Nor is it jealous insistence on the perpetuation of selfish local interests. What is involved is the preservation of self-government—leaving in the hands of the people of a particular region the right to regulate their own affairs in their own way. If they surrender power to the national government they have to submit to distant domination by authorities that are indifferent to local desires and needs. When the Federal government can regulate and control local problems, a small group of politicians in Washington can impose its ideas and wishes on the nation as a whole, and the people of particular regions who object have no alternative but to acquiesce.

· · · · · · · ·

One of the commonest criticisms of the American system of dual—and even triple—governments is that there is much duplication of effort due to the fact that the levels of government overlap, and that this requires increased personnel and implies avoidable waste.

This charge is of doubtful validity. In the first place, most of the officers of the different governments perform work which is not paralleled by others. The municipal, state and Federal administrations are, in the main, concerned with different activities and have different responsibilities. Such duplication as exists is more likely to be between county authorities and local or state units. Even these instances are comparatively rare and are confined to counties in which urban interests predominate.

It is also commonly asserted that as all three levels of government levy and collect taxes, there is much overlapping of this work. A moment's examination shows that this is a superficial judgment. With the possible exception of state and Federal income taxes, the imposition, collection, auditing and expenditure of the various types of taxes would require about as large a personnel and as much effort if done by one authority in the name of all three, as if done under the present system in which each different authority handles its own taxes. Mere similarity of function should not be mistaken for avoidable duplication. The creation of state police and Federal "G-men" has not served as a duplication of the work of local police.

243

It has supplemented it. Federal health officers perform different functions than do local health officers.

As a matter of fact, the lack of duplication of work between the various levels of government does not mean that there is no waste or superfluous employment in government today. Drastic reformation and modernization of state and municipal governments is imperative in the interest of efficiency, economy and sound administration. Many counties should be consolidated. Others—notably county governments in completely urbanized regions—should be abolished. Already some of the counties are revamping their own administrative methods and functions. Others need thorough overhauling.

But the objective in this housecleaning should be the deliberate strengthening of the local units and the enhancement of their powers of self-government. In particular, none of the functions which the local units can properly perform should be surrendered to larger units of government. This is as true of the cities and towns as of the counties; of the states as of the nation.

Only thus can self-government be maintained, and self-government is indispensable to the perpetuation of a society of free men devoted to the ideals of personal liberty, ultimate economic independence, and the more abundant life. Without self-government there can be no guaranty of personal freedom. When—as is now happening in countries where self-government has been abolished—men may be persecuted and exiled for reasons of state, or race, or religion, or political belief, true personal freedom cannot survive. Without self-government there can be no assurance of economic security—no guaranty that the state-supreme, in one of its several forms, will not supersede republican or democratic governments and impose on men such economic tasks and duties as the leaders of this state-all-powerful wish to have performed. The basis of self-government is local government. Local government, to be effective, must be responsible to the people of the locality—not to a distant and uninterested state or national capital.

The particular value of the Federal form is that it allows the fullest amount of diversity of local self-government within a framework of practical cooperation. To each unit it gives complete autonomy in local affairs, but in matters of common concern the units are served by a common government. This is why, of all the forms of government yet devised, federalism holds the greatest promise of meeting the changing conditions of changing times. It is essentially elastic, and hence is peculiarly well adapted to the administration of an enormous territory filled with a vast population. A half continent with 130 million inhabitants cannot be standardized and unified. By nature as well as by history there are many local diversifications. Federalism gives scope to these. At the same time it provides the machinery for the advancement of national interests—for the preservation of a standard currency, the maintenance of efficient forces of national defense, the balancing of the Federal budget and the perpetuation of the general welfare.

It is not without significance that the federal solution has recently been adopted in a modified form by the British Empire. The British Commonwealth of Nations is a group of autonomous states working together in the common interest but retaining full independence of control of their own internal affairs. This arrangement came into being because experience taught the British statesmen the clumsiness of too much centralized control. While the Commonwealth of Nations is not exactly parallel to the American Federal system, it is based on the dominant idea which moved the men who met in Philadelphia in 1787—the formation of an indestructible union composed of indestructible states.

America today is moving toward the kind of centralization that the British Empire has abandoned. In place of federalism, with its basic reliance on self-government and its provisions for local independence, the American system is being transformed into a unitary, centralized, all-powerful government. Light-heartedly, indifferently, suicidally, the American people are sacrificing the system under which the United States became a great republic. They have forgotten that the Federal way is the way of truly popular government, and that popular government is the very essence of modern democracy.

XVI

DISTRIBUTION AND COOPERATION

JUST AS in government the objective is to strengthen the self-dependence of local units, so in the economic field the objective is to break up financial and industrial concentrations and to increase the number of individual owners of the means of production.

To date only one method of checking the centralization of wealth and power has received wide support—to make government strong enough for it to dominate the great financial and industrial concerns. Some persons, like the radical socialists, want, as I have already indicated, government to own the means of production— to administer and control all business activities. Others wish to use the state as a great super-corporation, planning, coordinating and directing all the economic life of the country.

Apart from the fact that such a state-supreme would combine the evils of large business and large government organizations, its advocates ignore a principle which is as obvious as it is simple—that if centralization is an evil that must be overcome, the way to cure it is to decentralize, rather than to concentrate all power of all kinds in one vast super-organization, the government.

The arguments for decentralizing large business con-
solidations may be briefly recapitulated as follows: (1)
that the concentration of great economic power is socially
undesirable, as it places in the hands of a few rich men
the domination of the lives of millions; (2) that it is
economically inefficient—*i.e.*, that there is a point beyond
which size is unprofitable, and it then becomes advantageous to diffuse administration as well as to distribute
plants geographically; (3) that it is politically dangerous—that if free government is to be maintained, there
must be the widest possible diffusion of ownership of the
means of production, instead of concentration of economic control in the hands of a very small proportion of
the population, which, by its wealth and influence, can
dominate the government.

Decentralization was, until comparatively recently,
regarded as against nature. Men believed that growth
was irresistible, and that, in particular, the concentration of economic power was inevitable as a result of the
development of machinery. They pointed to the need for
establishing manufactures near sources of fuel like coal.
Steel, they said, could be more cheaply made in large
mills than in small ones. Railroads could only be operated by giant corporations because of the nature and
extent of their business.

But in recent years, technological development has
been doing much to facilitate the increase in the number
of small industries. Electric power can now be distributed

far and wide cheaply, thus eliminating the necessity of concentrating factories near accessible supplies of coal. Electrically operated plants are as mobile as the wires that connect them with the generator. Motor trucks now operate from one end of the country to the other, thus obviating complete dependence on the railroads.

The fact remains, nevertheless, that large business organizations are responsible for mass production and that mass production, in turn, is responsible for cheapening costs and hence making it possible for more people to buy more goods. If the large organizations are broken up, the advantages of cheap costs of production—so runs the argument of the advocates of centralization—must be abandoned, and we must return to the simpler economics of the pre-industrial era, giving up the comforts and luxuries provided by the modern industrial system.

Such an argument is superficial. The country neither could nor would do without the many improvements and comforts of life which are so largely the result of mass production. No sane person suggests returning to an earlier economic era. The real problem is to remodel the industrial structure so as to do away with the disadvantages of over-concentration without eliminating technological benefits.

Already many big corporations are voluntarily diffusing their factories and splitting up their organizations. They recognize that centralization is subject to the law of diminishing returns and that size can frequently be an actual handicap. Many competent observers of business developments expect the trend toward the break-up of large units to grow as business men realize the advantages of diffusion both in marketing and in obtaining labor.

It goes without saying, of course, that decentralization is not a hard and fast rule, applicable in all cases to all industries. There are certain types of business which neither can nor should be broken up. Of these the most obvious examples are the interstate railroads and the great telephone and telegraph systems. The nature of their services makes it inexpedient for them to decentralize. Coordination is indispensable in their day-to-day— and hour-to-hour—operation.

There are also types of business—like most of the "heavy industries" or "capital goods industries" that make machinery, cranes, dynamos, railroad equipment, etc.—in which small-scale organization is economically handicapped by technological difficulties. In such businesses centralized and more or less autocratic administration is unavoidable. Efforts should be made, however, to diffuse ownership as widely as possible among an ever-larger number of stockholders, notably among employees of the companies they work for—a policy followed with success by the great telephone companies.

But there are countless other businesses which can be and should be decentralized, either by breaking up big units into independent smaller organizations, or by introducing the principle of autonomy, leaving to local plants a large measure of self-determination without giving up the economies that mass purchasing and mass marketing make possible.

In this connection the cooperative movement deserves particular attention. Its greatest usefulness can be precisely in those occupations in which the need for decentralization is greatest—production and distribution of so-called consumers' goods: foodstuffs, clothing, furniture, drugs, and the countless other articles used by the mass of mankind in their ordinary day-to-day life. Unlike such industries as steel and the manufacture of tools and machinery, which depend on a few sources of raw materials, these consumers' goods industries draw their supplies of raw materials from many sources. The processors of foods use products that come from hundreds of thousands of different farms. The makers of clothing derive their cotton and wool from countless individual producers. In like manner the retailing of consumers' goods is undertaken by millions of individuals.

Experience in England, Sweden and elsewhere, shows that, beginning with local units dealing with local needs, the cooperative movement has spread through the federation of regional groups until large organizations have been built up, giving the members of cooperatives the benefits of size without imposing the toll of profits to individual or financial exploiters that is exacted under the traditional business system. The cooperatives have done this without in any way weakening or superseding the existing business structure. In Sweden they have managed to break private monopolies and greatly to reduce the price of all kinds of goods, whether or not handled by the cooperatives. The result has been to bring benefits to the Swedish consuming public and to place the business and economic system of Sweden on a sound basis. In Sweden government control of certain monopolies has also been undertaken. But there seems little doubt that the basic soundness of the Swedish economy is due largely to the strength and success of the cooperatives.

While it is unlikely that the cooperative movement in America can ever reach into and control the mass production of certain types of industries, here, as in Sweden, it can become an important force in fighting monopolies and price-fixing arrangements. Certainly it introduces into business a new element of popular influence which can be socially and economically valuable. By centralizing administration but decentralizing control, and by organizing for service rather than for the profit of the owners, cooperatives make it possible to preserve the benefits of large organizations without their disadvantages.

One of the chief merits of the cooperatives is that they are built from the ground up—that they are not imposed by the state or by selfish business interests. They have grown in response to popular interest, as an attempt to adjust the compulsions of a compact society to the needs of individuals. In many cases they started as a revolt against bad business practices. They have been motivated by self-protection and, where they have been wisely administered, they have brought substantial benefits to their members in the form of better and cheaper goods, not to mention contingent advantages in the form of savings accounts, insurance, etc.

The cooperative movement faces frankly the integrated nature of modern society. But it is in no sense antagonistic to capitalism. True, it strikes at the greatest weakness of modern capitalism—the abuses of the profit system. But it is based on the only principle which can preserve modern capitalism—spreading ownership of the means of production and distribution as widely as possible among the men and women who will use the goods that are produced, instead of, as at present, providing for the ownership of the means of production by a limited number of shareholders whose interests are solely in profits.

It is one of the paradoxes of the cooperative movement that, while it originated as a protest against capitalism, it has become in practice the greatest constructive alternative to socialism in any of its forms. It differs radically from state control in that it is based on fraternalism, not paternalism; on neighborly self-help, not on bureaucratic benevolence. It accepts the idea that individuals not only know what is to their own best interests but are able to work together in their own interests without government supervision or dictation. It seeks to unite neighbors in a common cause and to coordinate local units in the interest of all, leaving to each unit the largest amount of local control. Thrift and the acquisition of property are of its very essence.

In contrast to communism and socialism the cooperative movement repudiates the idea of a dominating class —the workers—and substitutes for it the classless interests of the consumers—all consumers. It rejects the doctrine of placing the workers as a class against the owners and employers as a class. Instead it seeks to coordinate the joint interests of consumers and workers by giving the consumers a direct interest in production. It seeks to bring to these consumer-owners the advantages of large-scale organization, and to eliminate the inherent antagonism between sellers and buyers by making the interests of both identical.

It is regrettable that in America the cooperative movement has met with much opposition from business men— especially from the great distributors. These have fought not only the consumers' cooperatives, but also the producers' cooperatives, such as the Dairymen's League, fruit-growers' associations, etc. That this is a short-sighted policy goes without saying, for the great need of all business men, large and small, is the elimination of the abuses of the profit system and the recognition of the common interest of all buyers in obtaining the best quality of goods at the lowest prices.

Cooperatives neither can nor should displace private business. But they can perform important services which may well help to stabilize the economic structure, and so help to make America not only a better place in which to live but a better place in which to conduct a business enterprise.

Valuable as the cooperative movement can be, it will not eliminate the need for government interference to correct business abuses and prevent unfair practices. Furthermore, government supervision and regulation of certain services, especially of those in which an element of monopoly is involved, is inevitable. Plausible arguments can be made for government ownership of the sources of power—the coal mines, oil supplies, and hydroelectric power resources. But the theoretical advantages of such a course are sure to be outweighed by the fatal danger that the politicians will use the control of these primary sources of power—which means the control of industry—to favor their friends and injure their enemies. In other words, the potential evils of such control are staggering.

In all considerations of the relation of government and industry it is important to realize that much depends on which level of government—Federal, state or local—assumes ownership or undertakes control, regulation, or operation. Only a moment's thought makes it clear that there are activities which, if performed by a local government, are proper and necessary but, if performed by the

Federal or even a state government, would be intolerable. The operation of a municipal sewage disposal plant, or of a local power plant, by the municipal government would obviously be admissible—always provided the service given were good, the rates fair, and no political favoritism were shown. But for the Federal government to operate municipal plants would be ridiculous.

Less clearly demarked is the line between the activities which may properly be performed by the states and by the Federal government. The states have in the past exercised all kinds of control over economic activities. If experience be a guide there is little, short of direct confiscation of private property, that state governments may not attempt, and even confiscation is conceivably permissible if a state government can make fair payments and devise means of seizure which fall within the technical definition of "due process of law." Logic would suggest that, except where the control of activities that are clearly of an interstate nature is involved, the authority of the states, rather than of the Federal government, should be extended when government intervention is indispensable.

At the risk of appearing to labor this point I stress the fact that governmental regulation *per se* is not the real issue, but rather, which of the various agencies of government shall do the regulating. While I know that this is a controversial problem, and that generalizations about it are likely to be meaningless, I insist that there is a fundamental difference of philosophy at issue—the philosophy of decentralization, with its faith in the ability of people to run their own affairs, and the philosophy of centralization, with its disbelief in the right as well as in the ability of people to govern themselves.

The states have, of course, often failed to pass such laws as reformers believe essential. For a good many decades numerous state governments were corrupt. This is one of the reasons why reformers have turned to the Federal government for action instead of to the states. Furthermore, no one can deny that the lack of uniformity between the policies of the different states toward labor and business has delayed social and economic reforms. These are obvious black marks against the states. But they are offset by the fact that the people of each state have the right to say how they shall be governed, and if one state wishes to make a thirty-hour week mandatory, and another wants to place few restrictions on business activities, the people of these states have a right to adopt such policies. To deprive them of this right in the name of uniformity or efficiency is to strike at the fundamental principle of self-government.

If, of course, the philosophy be accepted that the people of the different states do not know what is best for them—that they are incapable of managing their own affairs—then it is a farce to pretend to defend self-government. Federalism, cooperation, democracy, self-government must then go to the junk heap.

But those who have faith in the democratic principle are convinced that the safeguards of decentralization outweigh its disadvantages. They believe that the greater the diffusion of control the better for all concerned—that the evils of concentration, economic as well as political, are insuperable. They wish to see great business enterprises decentralized. They look toward a strengthening of local governments at the expense of the central power. They believe that, in business as in government, the creation of large units to take over functions which smaller units can perform just as well, should be discouraged. Only thus can concentration of power be diffused. Only thus can decentralization be achieved.

XVII

IN PURSUIT OF IDEALS

LET NO ONE delude himself into thinking that sound political and economic reforms can, by themselves, save American democracy. Unless there is a great spiritual and moral reawakening neither federalism, nor the restoration of property, nor the diffusion of ownership of the means of production, will be of much avail. Political and economic reforms are, of course, indispensable to the preservation of democracy—just as false political ideals and economic fallacies will surely destroy the priceless heritage of personal freedom. But such reforms cannot make democracy function effectively unless they are attended by a rebirth of self-reliance, a new faith in the God-given independence of spirit of every man, woman and child, and a new understanding of the eternal value of integrity, truth and honor. Without staunch moral standards in government and business as in personal affairs, life in America will be sterile.

The pioneers knew the worth of personal courage in the face of danger, of endurance under hardships and disappointments, of self-sacrifice and self-denial in the pursuit of ideals. They sensed that these are the attributes of free men in a free land. But today these qualities are questioned. Their worth is even denied. In their place idleness and apathy are defended, easy discouragement in the face of tribulations is applauded, and a new cult of dependence has won millions of adherents. These are the ideals of servile men—fit stuff on which to build a state-supreme.

America is spiritually atrophied—as is most of the rest of the world. But, in contrast to the rest of the world, there is still much health and vigor in the United States. It is the good fortune of the American people to be descended from the most aggressive and enterprising members of many European stocks. No finer human material exists on earth. Never before in any country has as large a proportion of the population been as well nourished. Never before have so many people had so many of the material advantages of life. Nowhere have the opportunities for personal development and expansion been so great—even since the world-wide depression.

Nor is this all. The resources of the United States are scarcely scratched. Vast reserves of those fuels and minerals which are the raw materials of modern industrial civilization are untouched and even unexplored. Inventive genius, unless stifled by political control, will surely find new sources of power, and new kinds of uses to which metals can be put. New machines will be devised, and new services and utilities will be provided through the intelligence and creative ability of new generations.

The material and physical basis of America is, therefore, sound. How cure its spiritual sickness?

In the old days the churches would have made the attempt. Today the churches—all the churches—fail to offer youth the kind of leadership that it craves. Some of them continue to hold, or even increase, their membership. But they have lost the power to inspire. The great lessons that they teach fall on indifferent ears.

At the same time the break-down of family life has removed the other most potent force of moral training—cooperative living under the influence of family tradition and discipline. Youth is thus floundering in a spiritually sterile sea. Undisciplined and uninspired by faith, youth feels lost and insecure. Confusion, disappointment, disillusion, have followed the collapse of old standards inevitable in the shattering of civilization by the World War. Seeking distraction and escape through the satisfaction of passing impulses, youth is experiencing the age-old emptiness of self-indulgence and self-preoccupation. The tragedy is that our young men and women do not realize that this emptiness is at the root of their dissatisfaction. Instead, they blame "society," and dream of a new world in which there will be still more idleness, still less responsibility, still easier escape from the compulsions of work and self-discipline.

To make matters worse the schools, through no particular fault of the educators but rather as a result of the levelling process inherent in mass education, have failed to provide a substitute for what the churches and the family used to give. The schools have tended to pamper youth—to make things as pleasant and as easy for the children as possible. The purpose has, of course, been admirable—to give the children the best that the community can offer. But education cannot be acquired without effort. Children do not learn the indispensable lesson of self-discipline when standards are set so low that the dull and lazy can "get by," when education is made into a form of distraction, and when they are relieved of the obligation of doing disagreeable tasks. It is not through ease and escape from effort and responsibility that strong men and women are formed.

Those who shaped our educational system did not, of course, realize how demoralizing were the forces that they unleashed. Not only have they encouraged a whole generation to look on hard work well and faithfully performed as futile, but they have led many school-children —and their parents—to believe that whatever forms of amusement and distraction the children crave should be furnished for them, gratis, by the state. It is for the children to ask—and to receive. In return, they are not expected to give anything—not even to show a proper appreciation for the generosity that has been showered upon them.

In thus relieving children of all sense of obligation the schools have reinforced a trend which began with the modernization of living conditions and the urbanization of so much of our population. Most children today are deprived of even such small responsibilities as a share in the household "chores"—carrying in the wood, milking the cows, filling the lamps. They are encouraged by their parents to feel "put upon" if the school bus does not come to the front door, saving them the inconvenience of walking a few blocks.

The contrast to the customs of the earlier America is striking—and illuminating. Apart from a minimum number of hours of home study during school term the children of today have nothing to do but to fight boredom. Home is dull, and hence to be avoided. Its few restraints are irksome. In the earlier days—and until very recently in parts of the West—children had their regular duties at home. One of my neighbors began milking cows at the age of 8, and when he was 10 years old was sent with his younger brother, aged 9, to drive fifty head of cattle down the California coast and bring back a string of horses. The two boys were given a week's supply of food and made their journey by themselves in what was then a wilderness. Can there be any doubt that they were infinitely more fortunate—and happier—than their contemporaries brought up without any such responsibilities? Was not this practical lesson in self-reliance worth more than years of pampering in a "modern" home?

The cult of dependence in place of independence has been vigorously supported by men high in authority in Washington. In the name of security and relief they have preached the doctrine that society owes every man a living, and that if he cannot get it as easily as he wants, it is the duty of the government to support him in idleness. They insist that those who will not work are entitled to the same reward as those who work—that the enterprising, the thrifty and the successful must turn over the result of their energy, thrift and success to those who are neither enterprising nor thrifty nor successful.

Plausible as this is—it can be distorted into compliance with the biblical injunction to be charitable—it is symptomatic of the soft thinking that has demoralized the nation. It shows a strange blindness to elemental concepts of personal justice. If a man works hard while his neighbor refuses to work, what possible claim has that idle neighbor on the worker? No amount of talk about the injustice of "privilege" can alter the fact that, to use the words of President Theodore Roosevelt, "there is no more mischievous form of privilege than giving equal rewards for unequal service and denying the great reward to the great service."

Equality of rewards has always been the objective of the defenders of the incompetent. By levelling rewards the lot of the inefficient and the lazy is improved. They benefit from the work and sacrifice of the toilers. This is all very well for the lazy and the incompetent, but would any one dare affirm that it is fair to the real workers, the real doers, the real producers?

As a corollary of this proposition, the old idea that

work is a curse and idleness a blessing has been transmuted into the doctrine that life should be made as easy as possible for every one. In so far as this is a reaction against excessive toil, unduly long hours of work, and the grinding routine of most occupations, it is understandable. To a certain extent it is even justifiable. But the doctrine has been so perverted that it strikes at the basis of society and has demoralized countless individuals.

What, after all, is the greatest curse of the country today? Idleness, and its bastard brother, irresponsibility. I do not refer alone to unemployment. Rather do I have in mind the enormous number of vacuous and stagnant hours with nothing to do which hang heavy on the youth of the land, and on many of their elders. They breed restlessness and discontent. They sap vitality and character. No amount of drugging by movies and radio, no amount of "burning up" the roads in automobiles, can give the satisfaction of work honorably performed.

As is usual, diagnosis is easier than prescribing the remedy. But the objective is clear, even if there be no simple answer to the question: "What can be done about it?" The great need is for fostering independence instead of dependence—for inculcating self-reliance, initiative and personal courage. To stand on one's own feet, to meet life without flinching, to play the game fairly, to hold fast to and live up to standards of integrity—these are still noble ideals. Furthermore, they foster self-respect and self-control, and self-control is at the root of character. Now as in all ages the men and women who possess their own souls, who can master themselves, who are brave and resolute and undefeated, are the inspiration of the race. To be as one of them is to be among the fortunate of the world. To emulate them is still the dream of healthy youth.

Together with a re-dedication to these ideals of character the American people need a new devotion to integrity. The term means something more than mere honesty. There is integrity of work as well as of word—doing a job thoroughly and well, for its own sake. Integrity strikes beneath the surface. It is concerned with the essence rather than the appearance. It disdains shoddy work—doing things "rather more or less." It is indifferent to popular acclaim. It scorns mere "getting by." Good work and honest thinking cannot exist without integrity.

In the inculcation of integrity the schools can play a part. They can do this through a greater emphasis on the "how" of school work. Today attention is centered on the "what." In other words, the importance of doing a job well and properly must be stressed, instead of merely getting it done. The method, rather than the results, must be emphasized—the difference between the right and the wrong way. This is at the basis of all good workmanship —and of all honorable living. Integrity is the arch-enemy of carelessness, sloppiness and deceit.

Because integrity is of the essence of true sportsman-ship, the proper development of sports can be of help to the schools in fostering personal discipline and character training. To obtain the best results, however, the empha-sis will have to be shifted from the "winning team" to the creation of as many teams as possible in each school. "Playing the game" must be stressed instead of victory. Attention will have to be centered on rules rather than on scores. The ideal is that each player shall do the best he can, regardless of the final outcome of the game—that he shall play cleanly and well, without "lying down on the game."

Not only learning to play a game well, but actually playing it fairly, develops initiative, self-control and endurance. There is the further advantage that the sort of physical training which is usual in preparation for sports is invaluable in the promotion of self-mastery. It is a form of practical idealism. Some sports, like skiing, call for a high degree of courage as well as of muscular skill, and have the further advantage that they are close to nature. Others, like small-boat sailing, develop alert-ness, attention and care. All alike emphasize the "how" —that there is a right way and a wrong way to do things. They put a premium on precision, self-discipline and integrity. Team play, in addition, shows the importance of cooperation and the advantages of well-disciplined organization in working toward a common end.

However valuable a new development of sports in the

schools can be, it will not relieve the parents of America of the duty of taking over again the difficult tasks of training their children and giving them a sense of responsibility. In recent years occupied parents have tended to leave most of this training to the schools. That the schools have failed must be clear to every one. This failure has thrust the responsibility back upon the parents—where, in truth, it belongs. Parents cannot dodge it by saying that they do not have the time to train their children. Europeans are just as busy as Americans—most of them, in fact, work longer hours—but they have never shirked the task of properly training their young.

In the earlier America, children were well disciplined. Among the Mormon people today the qualities of self-reliance, integrity and self-help are being most successfully fostered—among the old as well as the young. While this has been facilitated by the organization of the church as well as the good sense of its leaders, each family and each small community has taken its part in deliberately encouraging initiative, thrift and industry, and in striking at the curse of dependence and idleness. In Utah they are tired of "leaners"—as they call those men and women who prefer to let others support them rather than to support themselves. They help the self-helpers, and they preach to the young the importance of being able to stand on their own feet.

In thus restoring faith in the self-reliant and simple life the Mormons are reviving what was best in the earlier

American way. They are showing that Americans of today can profitably follow the example of their fore-bears. Without much money and without most of those luxuries which we have come to look upon as absolute essentials, the earlier Americans lived full lives. They enjoyed simple pleasures. They had an abundance of good food and drink, and they preserved standards of taste and discipline that stood their children in good stead. They worked hard—and enjoyed it. Theirs was essentially a simple life.

There were no class lines and no marked inequalities of wealth in the earlier America. Only when the great indus-trial and railroad fortunes were made in the last seventy years did extravagance and ostentation sweep over the country. False social standards were then built up about a group of people whose material acquisitiveness was ac-companied by cultural and spiritual sterility.

If the new rich had had less of the buccaneer spirit and more of a sense of civic responsibility they would have served their country—and themselves—better. But in-stead of leading in good government they contemptu-ously purchased political favors when these were profit-able. Instead of building sound family traditions, as the new rich had so long done in England, most of them contented themselves with trying to buy culture for their wives and daughters and trying to make country gentle-men out of their sons. The majority mistook display and extravagance for style. They confused the acquisition of works of art with a true appreciation of art. They thought that by buying books—but not reading them— they could acquire knowledge and wisdom. Some of them left splendid collections of paintings and fine libraries to the public. But neither the purchase, nor the ownership, of these paintings or books brought them true spiritual satisfaction. Many others gave endowments to hospitals and universities—with the express understanding that their names would be forever attached to these endowments. But the honorary degrees which they received from the grateful beneficiaries did not take the place of the quiet, sure culture that the men and women of the earlier generations had enjoyed. Only a few, like the Rockefellers, spent their money modestly and unostentatiously, ever alert to help good causes and to promote science and education.

Had the activities of the would-be fashionable rich concerned only themselves the evil that they did would have died with them. But many deliberately sought publicity for their ostentation. Others obtained it by studiously avoiding it. To the country at large they were represented as a moneyed aristocracy—as the leaders of American "society." Their antics, their charity balls, their extravagances, were no more futile and foolish than those of other plutocracies, but they served—rightly— to discredit the so-called "upper classes." The contrast of their shameful—and shameless—extravagance with the poverty of the workers played into the hands of political demagogues and gave opportunities to the preachers of class hatred to inflame the country against a system that made such a spectacle possible.

One of the many evil results of this is the gradual stratification of the people into classes. In the earlier America no rigid class lines existed. On this continent for the first time a society was built in which neighborliness and kindliness took the place of rank and snobbishness. But this classlessness is disappearing—largely because of the foolishness, selfishness and vanity of so many of the wives and heirs of the founders of great modern fortunes.

To make matters worse, as riches became identified in the popular mind with success, the American people sought to emulate those qualities which were conducive to the quick piling up of money. Acquisitiveness and cunning seemed more desirable—because more highly rewarded—than creativeness. Parasitism was at a premium. The purely material was preferred to the moral. So long as a man was rich, few held it against him if he had come by his wealth crookedly. It was thus natural that display came to be regarded as a badge of merit. The unsuccessful felt impelled to hide their failure by a false front of material ostentation. Sham took the place of sincerity. Hollowness and deceit became the accepted standards.

That America has survived the degradation of its great financial and industrial "kings" and "barons" and the demoralization of the mad scramble for material prosperity is a proof of its essential soundness. So also is the fact that it has survived the inundation by a horde of immigrants from Central and Eastern Europe bringing traditions of personal and political life that were at variance with those of the earlier Americans. In no sense were these people inferior—in fact, in many ways they were superior to the earlier immigrants. But the newcomers were so different that their standards and those of the natives often clashed, and on both sides intolerance developed. To make matters worse, their children, in their eagerness to appear American, seized on all the superficial—and usually the worst—American characteristics and then flaunted these in the faces of their parents. The result was to rend immigrant families and to cut off the children from the traditions of the old country before they assimilated those of the new.

That this has been infinitely hard on them as on the country goes without saying. The marvel is that, despite these handicaps and the race prejudices which America inherited from Europe, the many stocks have so well amalgamated. In only one particular is the cleavage great—and important: that most of the immigrants from Central, Eastern and Southern Europe lacked the tradition of self-government which was brought to this continent by the peoples of British and Northern European stocks, and that as a result, nearly half of the population of the United States today has no keen sense of the meaning of self-government. Without such a tradition the preservation of democracy is difficult, for popular government depends on a deeply rooted sense of self-restraint and cooperation—qualities which must be ingrained if self-government is to be stable.

Today the American people are infinitely better off than is the rest of the world. They have a rich land—a beautiful land. Some of it has been desecrated, but much retains its original splendor. They have a great—but neglected—tradition—the tradition of self-reliance of those stalwart men and long-suffering women who conquered a continent and tamed the wilderness. It is their supreme good fortune that, in addition, they have inherited a form of government which has given opportunities never before offered to any other people to grow and develop in almost unrestricted freedom, unhampered by lords and overlords and little scathed by war on their own territory.

Unfortunately, most Americans do not know the value of their heritage. They have lost their perspective. Misled by the glitter of this mechanical age, most of them are no longer content with simple, homely things. The artificial has lured them away from the natural. Mass production has enhanced their dependence on things—on tools and toys and gadgets. They look to the radio, the movies and automobiles to stifle their boredom. Few of them know the satisfaction of the elemental things that their forebears loved when they lived close to the land—the sun, sky and sea, and trees and flowers and birds.

But the American tradition is not yet extinguished. There are still millions of men and women who cherish what was best in the American way. They have not been misled by the slack standards of a society which measures success in terms of wealth instead of worth, and prefers ease to effort. In fact, their example proves that the old ideals are still richly vital.

On these people of modest means but proud traditions rests the duty of resuming the burden of leadership in community affairs, of supporting sound political and economic reforms, of attacking the false gods of wealth, idleness, irresponsibility and dependence. If, in business as in the home, they fight on with new courage for decency and integrity; if they honor their children by taking the pains to train them in self-discipline; if they attempt to be fair and to be brave; if they stifle envy, scorn misrepresentation, refuse to accept what is not justly theirs, and respect others as they respect themselves;—then no one need fear for the future of America. Not by acts of Congress nor by Constitutional amendments can the country be saved, but by the cooperative determination of millions of Americans that the United States shall be in the future as it was in the past—the home of self-reliant, independent, brave and generous men and women. There must be a new faith in the old ideals— spiritual as well as political—if the dreams of those who founded and helped build America are to come true.